David Cheetham spent mar [illegible] of his native Derbyshire and leadi[illegible] navia before he and his family came [illegible] in 1973.

David is also an experienced cyclist, and in addition to spending a great deal of time exploring the lanes and villages of Somerset has completed the journey from Lands End to John O'Groats, toured in France and taken part in the London to Brighton Charity run. He believes that Somerset is a most beautiful county and ideal territory for cyclists of all ages and ability.

These rides have something for everyone, and the completion of one or more of them will add to the list of enthusiasts for this special part of the British Isles.

CYCLING IN SOMERSET

DAVID CHEETHAM

DOVECOTE PRESS

First published in 1994 by the Dovecote Press Ltd
Stanbridge, Wimborne, Dorset BH21 4JD

ISBN 1 874336 25 3

Phototypeset in Bembo by
The Typesetting Bureau, Wimborne, Dorset
Printed and bound by Biddles Ltd
Guildford and King's Lynn

CONTENTS

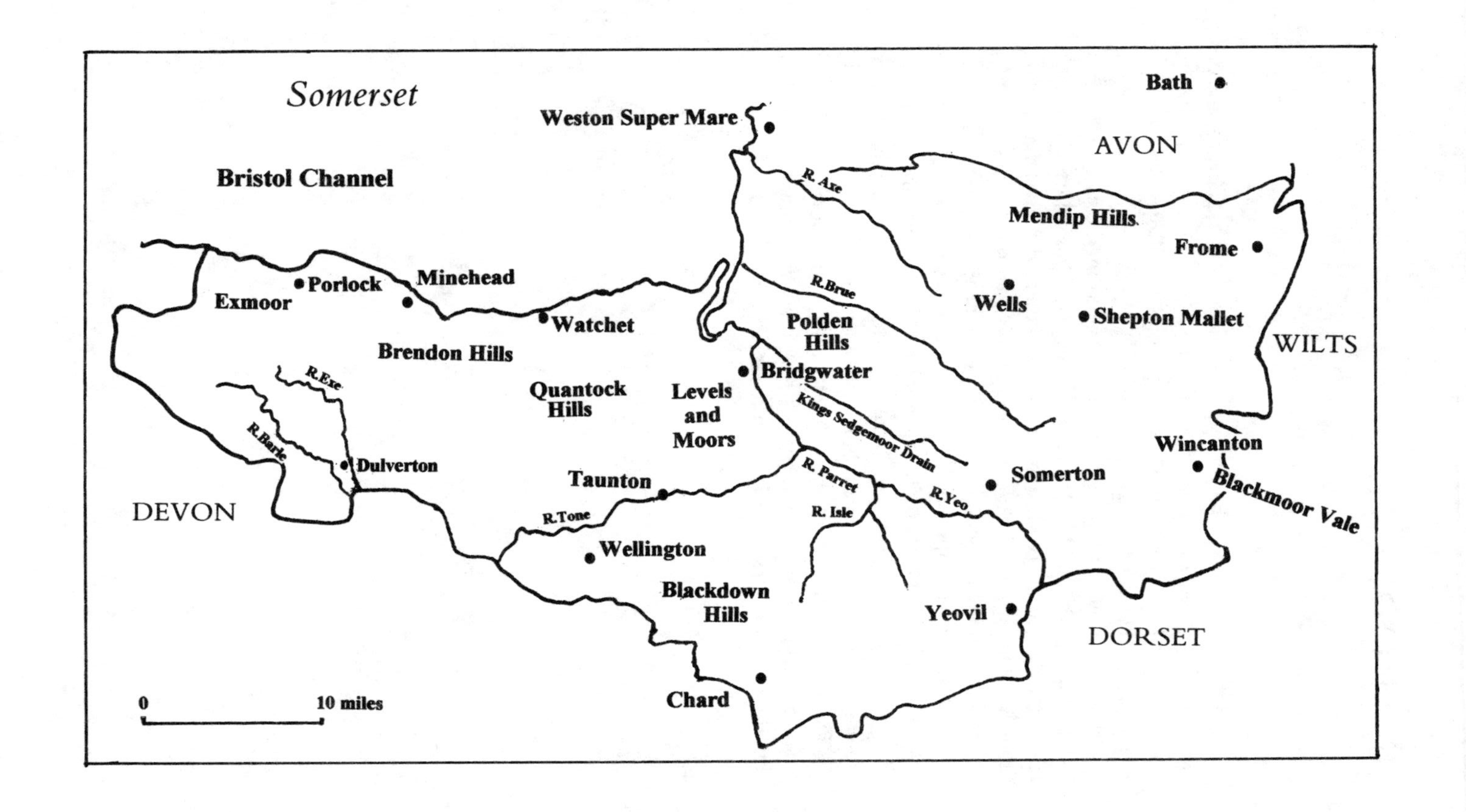
Somerset
Bath
Weston Super Mare
AVON
Bristol Channel
R. Axe
Mendip Hills
Frome
Minehead
Porlock
Exmoor
R.Brue
Wells
Shepton Mallet
Watchet
Polden
Hills
WILTS
Brendon Hills
Bridgwater
R.Exe
Quantock
Hills
Levels
and
Moors
Kings Sedgemoor Drain
Wincanton
R.Barle
Dulverton
R. Parret
Somerton
Blackmoor Vale
Taunton
R.Yeo
DEVON
R.Tone
R. Isle
Wellington
Blackdown
Hills
Yeovil
DORSET
Chard
0
10 miles

INTRODUCTION

Discovering Somerset by bicycle is a most memorable experience, and this series of rides takes the cyclist through landscapes of outstanding beauty, pleasant country towns rich in history, picturesque villages of great charm and populated by friendly people.

In Somerset there is a wide variety of terrain, from the stark hill country of the Mendip Hills in the north, to the Quantock Hills, which stretch from near Watchet on the coast, to a position straddling Bridgwater and Taunton. In addition the Blackdown Hills look down on the town of Wellington, whilst the Brendon Hills rise above Minehead and lead to Exmoor.

Between the Mendips and the Quantocks there lie the expansive Somerset Levels, interrupted only by the Polden Hills and the famous Glastonbury Tor. In contrast, the farmlands of South Somerset comprise gently rolling hills and remote hamlets linked by quiet lanes.

The rides cover each of these distinct regions of Somerset and reveal their different characteristics. Three briefly cross the Somerset boundary, but this does not detract from the Somerset element.

General comments about the routes

The routes never exceed 40 miles, the optimum distance for a cycle journey to be one of exploration and discovery rather than one of short stops and a chase for home. Each ride begins from a car park in a main town or village in the area to be covered.

A detailed map is provided for each route, taken from the appropriate Ordnance Survey Landranger Sheet(s) from the selection 172, 173, 181, 182, 183, 193 and 194. The rides are divided into stages, each described in detail with brief notes on points of interest. The details of the Ordnance Survey map(s) used, the grid reference for the starting point for the ride, the mileage, and an approximate realistic cycling time are given.

For a smooth ride in unfamiliar territory it is recommended that careful reading of the route and map is made before starting out on the journey.

Guide lines for a day‘s cycle ride

For the rides described in this book it is desirable but not essential to have a lightweight touring bicycle of the correct size with a wide range of gears, the necessary accessories, a good and comfortable saddle and a strong, waterproof saddle bag. The bicycle, whatever the type, should be in sound mechanical condition.

Before the journey make sure that the tyres are pumped up to the pressure recommended by the manufacturers and the height of the saddle is correct.

Carry one or two spare inner tubes, a puncture repair outfit and a small kit of tools which should include tyre leavers, tapernose pliers, screwdriver, a combination spanner and Allen keys if appropriate. Check that the bicycle pump is in good working order and make sure that you know how to repair a puncture or replace an inner tube.

If you will be returning home late in the evening, particularly in the autumn or winter months, check that the rear reflector is clean, that there‘s a red rear light and a strong and effective white light in front.

Don‘t set out on an empty stomach and be sure to take a water bottle and a small supply of food, which may be selected from fruit, chocolate, fruit cake or bread with cheese or ham.

Clothing

Choose clothes that are comfortable and can accommodate any change in the weather. It is essential to keep warm when stopping for a break and advisable to wear bright clothing for safety. Remember cold weather and insufficient clothing can lead to cramp.

In wet conditions a light weight waterproof jacket and trousers will provide protection against the worst weather. Breathable waterproofs are now available.

Road Safety

It is recommended that all cyclists should take note of the safety rules for cyclists in the Highway Code particularly in respect of the wearing of helmets. To these may be added the following points when travelling on the Somerset routes.

1. Be watchful for farm vehicles and animals when cycling along the quiet lanes.

2. Take extra care when cycling along muddy lanes whether the road surface is wet or dry.

3. Dismount and walk, if nervous, when descending steep gradients.

4. Ride carefully along lanes where the roadside hedges have been trimmed. The thorns or small sharp clippings can puncture the tyre very easily.

5. Give way to the motorist in narrow lanes.

6. Wear sunglasses or goggles in summer to provide protection from the sun, dust particles and midges.

7. The public houses that are included on each route act as landmarks and places of refreshment for soft drinks and either sandwiches or a meal. It is emphasised in the Highway Code that a cyclist must not ride under the influence of alcohol.

Summary of the Rides

Ride	Terrain	Distance	Start	Best Attributes
1	moderate	26.5	Shepton Mallet	Nunney Castle, Mells
2	moderate	13.0	Wells	Priddy, Wookey Hole
3	moderate	23.0	Cheddar	coastal views, contrasting landscapes
4	moderate	31.0	Frome	rivers and villages
5	easy	23.5/26.0	Wincanton	pastoral scenery
6	moderate	14.5/31.0	Bruton	woodland and hills
7	easy	36.0/38.0	Somerton	flat lands, hill villages
8	easy	23.5	Glastonbury	the Levels
9	easy	23.0	Langport	the Levels, historic villages
10	easy	33.0	Street	Glastonbury Tor, Wells
11	easy	21.0	Wedmore	coastal, Brent Knoll hill fort
12	easy	34.0	Yeovil	hamstone villages
13	moderate	37.0	Chard	farmland, villages
14	easy	34.0	Ilchester	South Cadbury hill fort
15	easy	34.0	Ilminster	countryside, villages
16	difficult	33.0	Ilminster	valleys and hills
17	difficult	30.0	Bridgwater	remote lanes, hill villages, Fyne Court
18	easy	24.0	Williton	coast, hills
19	moderate	23.0	Wellington	farmland, Wellington Monument
20	moderate	34.0	Taunton	quiet lanes, villages
21	moderate	25.0	Taunton	hills, beach, steam train ride
22	moderate	14.0	Watchet	sea coast, scenic views
23	difficult	28.0	Wiveliscombe	lake, hills, remote villages
24	moderate	24.0	Minehead	Selworthy, Allerford
25	difficult	28.0	Dulverton	moorland, wooded valleys

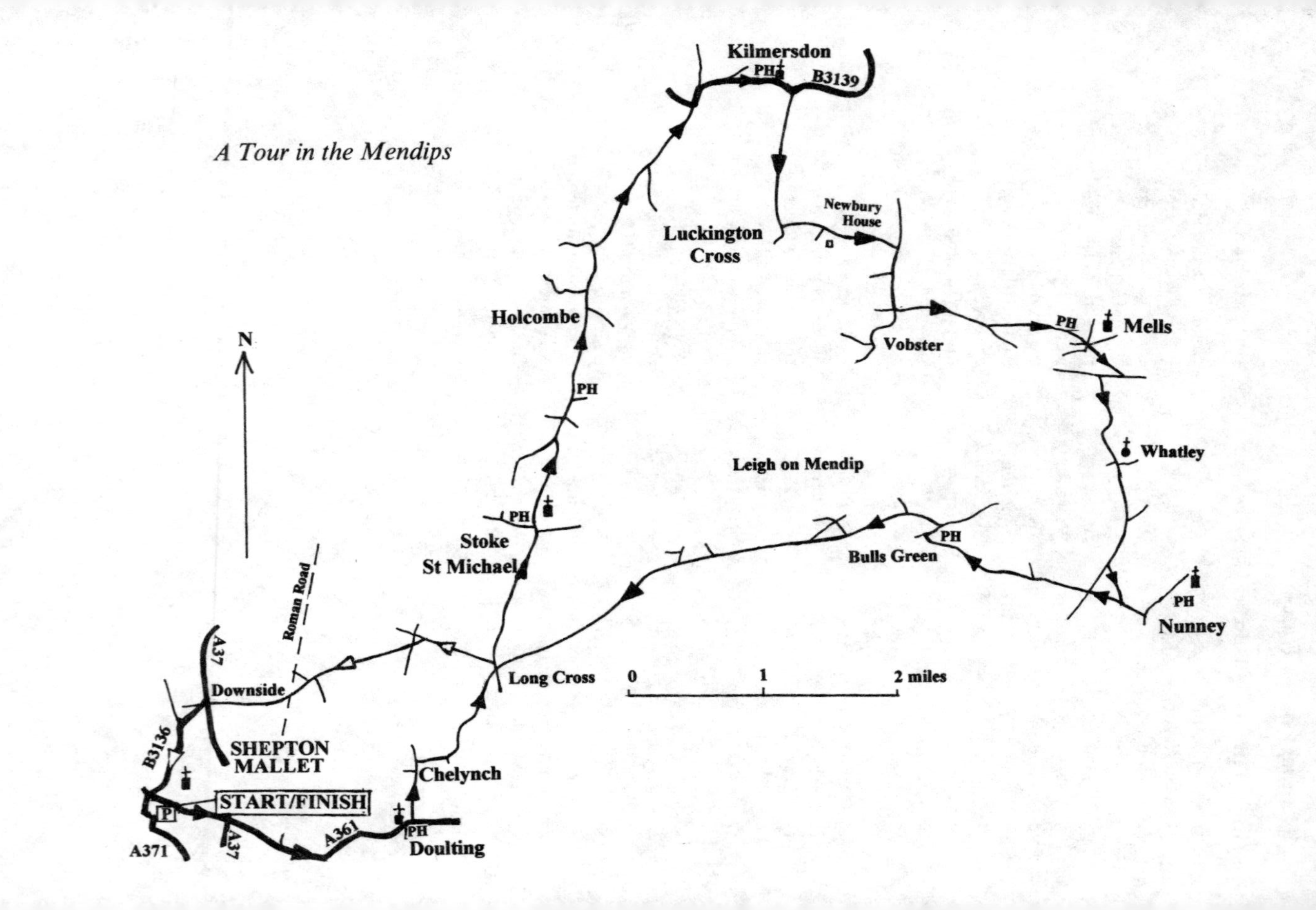
A Tour in the Mendips
N
Kilmersdon
PH
B3139
Luckington Cross
Newbury House
Holcombe
Vobster
PH
Mells
Whatley
Leigh on Mendip
PH
Stoke St Michael
Bulls Green
Nunney
Roman Road
Long Cross
0
1
2 miles
A37
Downside
B3136
SHEPTON MALLET
Chelynch
START/FINISH
P
A371
A37
A361
Doulting

RIDE 1

A TOUR IN THE MENDIPS

Distance: 26.5 miles.
Journey time: approximately 5-6 hours.

Route Description

The route begins in Shepton Mallet and takes the form of a figure eight, passing through an area of the Mendip Hills, with its isolated farmsteads, small hamlets and villages. Agriculture is the dominant industry but the quarrying of limestone is always in evidence and its influence is seen in the many stone-built houses and field walls.

Apart from the first two miles of the journey, along the A361 to Doulting, the tour uses the minor roads through Chelynch, Stoke St Michael and Kilmersdon on its way to Mells and Nunney. The return to Shepton Mallet from Nunney is through pleasant countryside to Long Cross and from there to Downside and Shepton Mallet.

Start: (O.S. Landranger sheet 183, Grid reference ST615434)

From the Public Car Park in Old Market Road, Shepton Mallet, turn right and then right again at the mini-roundabout, onto the A361 to Frome. At the A37 cross directly and continue straight ahead to Doulting. Just beyond the Charlton House Hotel the road bears left uphill for a half mile to Doulting. The church on the left and the Manor farm on the right stand prominently at the entrance to the village. In the village the Abbey Barn Inn is on the right of the main road.

Points of interest

Doulting: The local quarries supplied oolite limestone for Wells Cathedral and Glastonbury Abbey. The 17th century tithe barn Manor Farm can be viewed from the Abbey Barn Inn.

Stage 1 Doulting – Chelynch – Stoke St Michael – Holcombe

From the Abbey Barn Inn continue for a short distance along the A361 and take the first turn on the left for Chelynch, a small hamlet where the most prominent building is the Poachers Pocket Inn. From the Inn follow the road round to the right and continue to a road junction (Long Cross). Turn left to Stoke St Michael 1.5 miles away.

The road descends past a large quarry into Stoke St Michael. Take the road to the right of the Knatchbull Arms, passing the church and continue on to a junction. Turn right to Holcombe and climb up through the village for half a mile. At the summit there are clear views of Midsomer Norton and

Radstock.

Points of interest

Stoke St Michael: Knatchbull Arms, a fine example of 17th century architecture.

Holcombe: the parents of Captain Robert Falcon Scott, the Antarctic explorer are buried in the old church.

Stage 2 Holcombe – Kilmersdon – Mells – Nunney

From the summit at Holcombe continue to the B3139. Turn right to Kilmersdon. The church of St Peter and St Paul is at the bottom of the hill leading down to the village. Pass through the village (Jolliffe Arms on the left) to where the B3139 bears left. Turn right along the signposted Hoares Lane and follow the road up to Luckington Cross. Turn left to Mells passing Newbury House on the right. After one mile turn right at the junction towards Vobster. At the next crossroads turn left and then left again at the next junction into Mells. The village is worth exploring and refreshments can be obtained from the Talbot Inn.

Cycle through the village past the War Memorial and up the hill ahead to a junction. Turn right and then first left to Nunney. The spire of the church at Whatley can be seen directly ahead. Within about 1.5 miles turn left at the signpost to Nunney. The first sudden view of the castle and church is quite spectacular.

Points of interest

Mells: 15th century church, Elizabethan manor, 15th century Talbot Inn, village lock-up, alms houses and street of 15th century houses.

Nunney: the Castle, All Saints Church and Market Cross.

Stage 3 Nunney – Shepton Mallet

Leave Nunney by the same entry road but only as far as the top of the hill. Turn first left by the Castle farm. Go straight ahead at the next crossroads and continue along the road as it winds to Bulls Green. Turn right and then left at the road junction in Bulls Green and cycle four miles without any deviation to Long Cross.

At the Longcross crossroads turn right and then immediately left along the signposted Wells road. Take the first turn on the left to Shepton Mallet. Keep straight on at the next junction and continue to the A37. The road into Shepton Mallet is directly opposite, passes under the viaduct and continues to the A361 at a roundabout. Pass over the roundabout to the Car Park on the left.

Meals and refreshments are available near the Market Cross.

Points of interest

Shepton Mallet: the Parish Church of St Peter and St Paul, the Market Cross, the Prison, the Rectory/Strode's Grammar School.

RIDE 2

A SHORT RIDE FROM WELLS

Distance: 13 miles.
Journey time: approximately 3-4 hours.

Route Description
On this tour, from Wells to Priddy and Wookey Hole, the effort needed in climbing from Wells to the summit of the Mendips is amply rewarded by a feast of historic and geographic gems. There is sufficient time to explore Wells, the tumuli on the Mendips, the caves of Wookey Hole and to linger awhile to admire and absorb the scenic beauty on route.

Start: (O.S. Landranger sheet 182, Grid reference ST545454)
On leaving the car park in Princes Road turn right into Princes Road and pass through the traffic lights to a mini-roundabout. Turn right along Chamberlain Street and at the end of this one-way street bear left to another mini-roundabout and follow the A39 along New Street. Take the first turning on the left into Ash Lane, and almost immediately turn right along the clearly marked Old Bristol Road which is steep in parts, winds uphill and from which there are excellent views. A little way ahead the road flattens out, takes a sharp right turn and descends before climbing to the summit at 2.7 miles.
Points of interest
Wells: the 12th century Cathedral, together with the moated Bishop's Palace, the 14th century Vicars Close and the Market Place form the historic centre of the city. The Museum and Information Centre are important sources of information on the whole of the tour area.

Stage 1 Wells – Priddy
At the summit the surrounding countryside is moorland contained within boundaries of stone walls. From here the road is straight and falls gently to a crossroads. Refreshments can be obtained at the Hunters Lodge Inn. Cross the road and continue with Stockhill Forest on the right and scrubby moorland on the left, the surface of which is riddled with hillocks and hollows in a most irregular manner. This is an area where lead was once mined and is now called the Priddy Mineries Reserve, a site of special interest because of the heath and the bog vegetation and the lead tolerant plants on the spoil banks. For more information see the Information Board at the side of the road.

The road rises in a series of steps to a crossroads. Turn left, pass the Miners Arms, and follow the road to Cheddar on the B3135. The Priddy Stone Circles are in a field on the right at approximately 500 yards from the

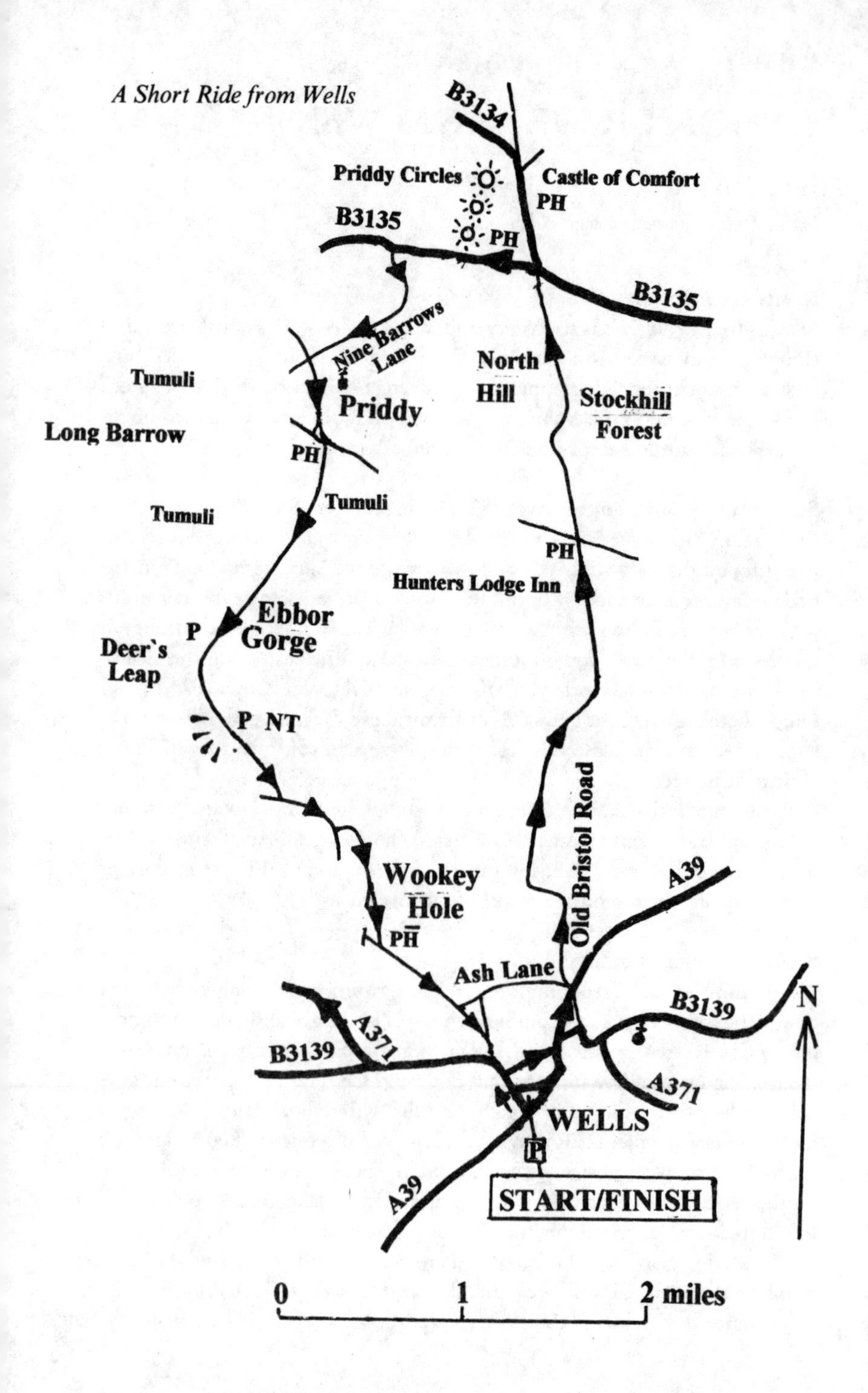
A Short Ride from Wells
B3134
Priddy Circles
Castle of Comfort
PH
B3135
PH
B3135
Nine Barrows
Lane
North
Hill
Tumuli
Priddy
Stockhill
Forest
Long Barrow
PH
Tumuli
Tumuli
PH
Hunters Lodge Inn
Ebbor
Gorge
P
Deer`s
Leap
P NT
Old Bristol Road
Wookey
Hole
PH
A39
Ash Lane
N
B3139
A371
B3139
A371
WELLS
P
START/FINISH
A39
0
1
2 miles

crossroads, and to the left on North Hill there are the Nine Barrows. Continue and turn left just before an S-bend into a narrow lane. It passes through a copse of trees and is edged for a short distance with wooden posts approximately 2 feet high. There is no name sign in this lane but it leads down to Priddy and is called Nine Barrows Lane.

A look at the map will show the extent to which this area was used for burials in ancient times. The lane winds downhill to a triangle of grass with a signpost. Take the road to the left towards Wells which leads down to the centre of Priddy. The pile of sheep hurdles for which the village is renowned is on the village Green to the right, with the New Inn on the far side.

Points of interest

Priddy: the highest village in Somerset (800 feet) and an ancient lead mining settlement. It is a prehistoric site with many tumuli, Priddy Nine Barrows and Priddy Stone Circles being amongst the most prominent ones. The bundle of hurdles on the Green is said to ensure the rights of the villagers to hold an annual fair, a custom dating back to 1348.

Stage 2 Priddy – Wookey Hole – Wells

Take the unsignposted single-track road to the left of the New Inn, passing the Queen Victoria Inn on the left. The road eventually passes a viewing point called Deer's Leap, with a car park and picnic area. This is one of the best viewing points in Somerset with views from the Wiltshire border in the east to the Bristol Channel and Exmoor in the west. Glastonbury Tor can also be seen. The view on a clear day is truly breathtaking.

From this point onwards care must taken because of the steepness of the narrow winding road and cars that use it. Further down the road there is a National Trust picnic area and another viewing point. From here there is a sharp S-bend and the road then runs down to a straight flat stretch to a signpost at a junction. Bear left down into the village of Wookey Hole. There is a car park on the right in which there are excellent refreshments and toilet facilities. Tickets can be purchased here for a tour of the caves and the Paper Mill.

To return to Wells continue through the village past Wookey Hole Inn on the left and follow the signs to the City of Wells. Turn left at the A371 and travel through Wells to the car park in Princes Road.

Points of interest

Wookey Hole: famous for the caves which have yielded the remains of rhinoceros, reindeer, wolf, and evidence of their habitation by early man. The River Axe flows through magnificent underground chambers. Another equally interesting attraction is the Victorian Paper Mill.

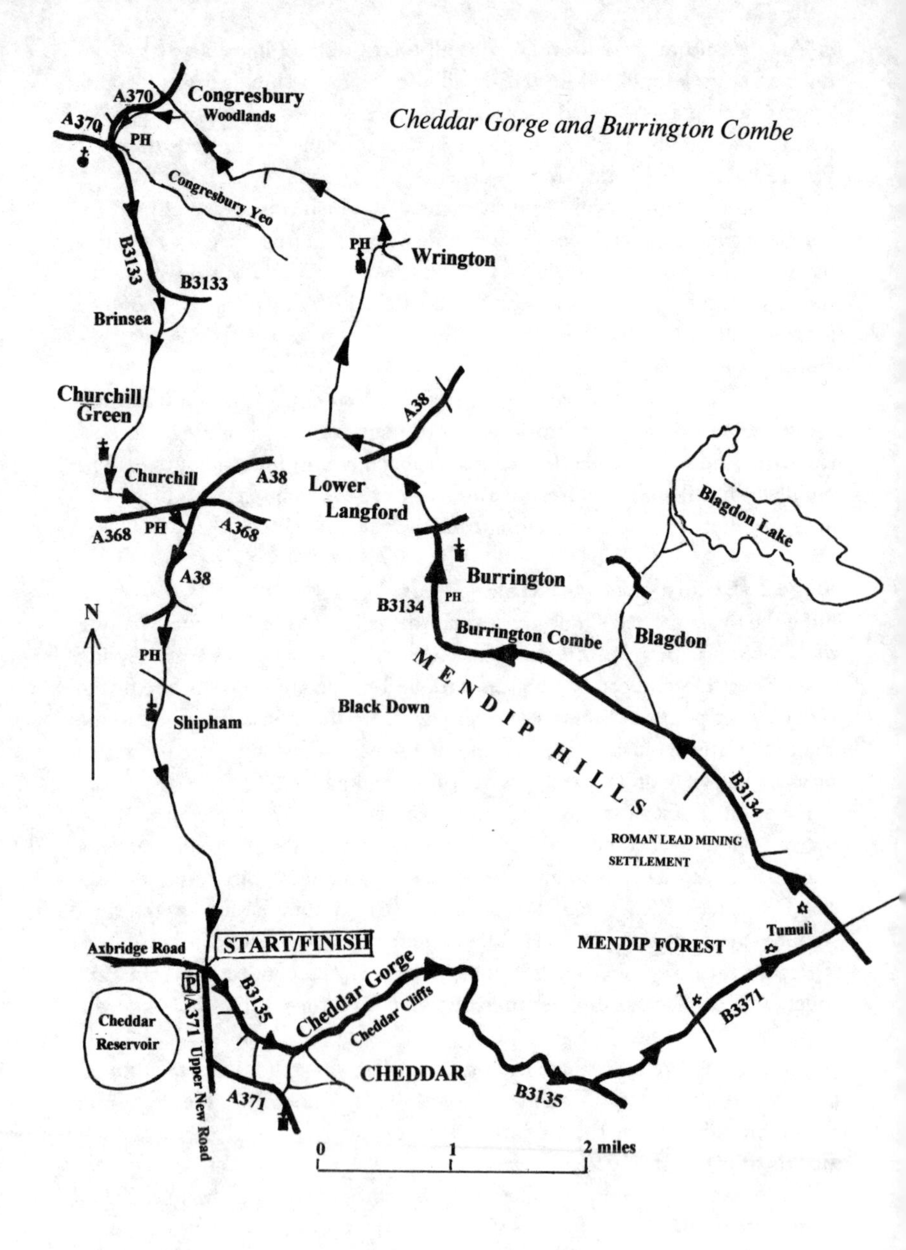

Cheddar Gorge and Burrington Combe
A370
A370
Congresbury
Woodlands
PH
Congresbury Yeo
B3133
B3133
Brinsea
Churchill
Green
Churchill
A38
A368
PH
A368
A38
N
PH
Shipham
PH
Wrington
Lower
Langford
A38
Burrington
B3134
PH
Burrington Combe
Blagdon
Blagdon Lake
MENDIP HILLS
Black Down
B3134
ROMAN LEAD MINING
SETTLEMENT
Tumuli
MENDIP FOREST
B3371
START/FINISH
Axbridge Road
P
A371
Upper New Road
Cheddar
Reservoir
B3135
Cheddar Gorge
Cheddar Cliffs
CHEDDAR
A371
B3135
0
1
2 miles

RIDE 3

CHEDDAR GORGE AND BURRINGTON COMBE

Distance: 23 miles.
Journey time: approximately 6 hours.

Route description

This is a tour in an area of contrasting landscapes. It begins in Cheddar with a climb up through the Cheddar Gorge on a winding road, flanked on each side by towering walls of limestone rock, where grass, gorse and bracken compete for territory. The descent from the Mendips through the smaller, shallower gorge of Burrington Combe leads to the pasture land of Lower Longford, a geographical feature which persists throughout the area. It includes Wrington, Congresbury and Churchill where the Mendips are scaled once more to the village of Shipham, with its view of the Bristol Channel and the island of Flat Holm. From here a steep descent is made back to Cheddar.

The hills encountered on this journey are not intimidating.The exhilarating descents through Burrington Combe and from Shipham to Cheddar more than compensate for the effort in climbing up through Cheddar Gorge and the hill on the A38 near Churchill.

Start: (O.S. Landranger sheet 182, Grid reference ST447545)

Turn right from the exit/entry of the Car Park on the Axbridge Road and at the corner with Upper New Road, cross the junction to join the B3135 (also Axbridge Road). This leads through the village of Cheddar and up the Gorge to the B3371. Although the ride up the Gorge looks steep there is only one point, the horseshoe bend, where the road is awkward. The remainder of the journey is a gradual climb to the B3371. Follow the B3371 (signposted to Bristol and Bath) to the B3134. Turn left to Burrington. Approximately 2 miles from here the heather-covered moors of Black Down can be seen to the west and fine views to the east towards Butcombe and Nempnett Thrubwell beyond Blagdon Lake. The ride down Burrington Combe is both long and exhilarating but care must be taken. At the bottom of the gorge light refreshments or main meals can be obtained at the Burrington Free House, more restaurant than public house.

Points of interest

Burrington Combe: Avelin's Hole, a large cave on the east side of the combe, discovered in 1797, and found to contain many skeletons of human beings who lived 10,000 years ago.

Stage 1 Burrington Combe – Lower Langford – Wrington – Congresbury

From Burrington Free House continue downhill to the A368. Turn right and then almost immediately left to Lower Langford passing Langford Court on the left. At the A38 turn left and then immediately right onto the minor road into the village. Travel through the village and take the first road on the right to Wrington, 1.5 miles away. In Wrington, pass the church on the left before turning sharp right into Broad Street, the main shopping area. Richards' Store on the left provides a wide range of cycling accessories. At the head of Broad Street turn sharp left at the Golden Lion and follow the road to Congresbury, 2.25 miles away. To avoid the busy A370 take the last turning on the left, (opposite 'Woodlands') about 350 yards before the junction with the A370. See the accompanying map. This joins a second minor road which leads from the A370 to the B3133 near traffic lights and the Ship and Castle Inn Continue left along the B3133 for approximately 1 mile and where the road bears left, take the right turn to Brinsea and Churchill.

Points of interest

Lower Langford: interesting village well worth exploring.

Wrington: once an important part of Glastonbury Abbey's great estate.

Congresbury: noted for the hill fort overlooking the village

Stage 2 Churchill – Shipham – Cheddar

From Brinsea follow the road through Churchill Green to the T-junction with the Sandford to Churchill road. Turn left along Font Street and continue through the village and bear left at the junction with the A368. After about 200 yards turn right by the Nelson's Arms Inn in Skinners Lane. Follow this road and turn right at the A38. Climb 0.75 miles to the signpost to Shipham just beyond the right hand bend at the top of the hill. Care should be exercised on this busy road.

Turn left off the A38 to Shipham, climbing a slight hill before descending into the centre of the village. Refreshments can be obtained from either the Miner's Arms or the Penscot Farmhouse and Hotel. Although the hill out of the village towards Cheddar is short and steep, the reward is an excellent view of the Bristol Channel and the island of Flat Holm, followed by a long downhill run to the finishing point at the car park in Cheddar

Points of interest

Churchill: early ancestral home of the Churchill family. The village is overlooked by Dolebury hill fort.

Shipham: formerly a centre of calamine mining providing zinc for the Bristol brass industry.

Cheddar: a medieval town famous for its cheese and caves. The caves contain wonderful stalactites and stalagmites and are worth a visit. Gough's Cave is known to have been inhabited by man almost 14,000 years ago.

RIDE 4

ALONG THE RIVER FROME

Distance: 31 miles.
Journey time: approximately 5-6 hours.

Route Description

The River Frome flows through the town of Frome and becomes part of the boundary between Somerset and Wiltshire. It eventually joins the River Avon on the county boundary between Avon and Wiltshire.

The tour begins in Frome and runs alongside the river to the delightful village of Lullington where the ride and river distance themselves from one another before meeting again briefly at Farleigh Hungerford. From there the ride leaves Somerset and moves into Wiltshire passing through Westwood, Bradford-on-Avon, Winsley and Limpley Stoke, to reach Freshford in Avon overlooking the meeting of the two rivers. The final stage to Somerset and Norton St Philip is via Hinton Charterhouse (Avon), and from there through the narrow winding lanes to Laverton, Buckland Dinham, Great Elm and back to Frome.

This journey passes through beautiful countryside and charming villages with many lovely views, particularly over the valley where the Rivers Frome and Avon meet.

Start: (O.S. Landranger sheets 172,173 and 183, Grid reference for sheet 183 ST780482)

This ride begins from the car park in North Parade (B3090), Frome. From the car park exit turn left onto the B3090 and then take the first right along Welsh Mill Road. The wide road descends and runs alongside, but some distance from the River Frome and the railway, both on the left.

The road takes a winding course leading to Innox Hill and beyond before crossing the river to a junction. Turn right towards Oldford. Cross the river again and continue following its course through open country to the B3090. At the Give Way sign turn left and almost immediately left again to Lullington (1 mile). The road passes the Eden Vale Creamery over to the right and crosses the River Frome again. This is a quiet area free from traffic and lined with handsome trees. On the outskirts of Lullington turn right to Woolverton (1.5 miles) opposite the castle-like entrance to Orchardleigh Park on the left.

Points of interest

Frome: historic and attractive market town on the banks of the River Frome with quaint narrow streets. Cheap Street is the best known with its

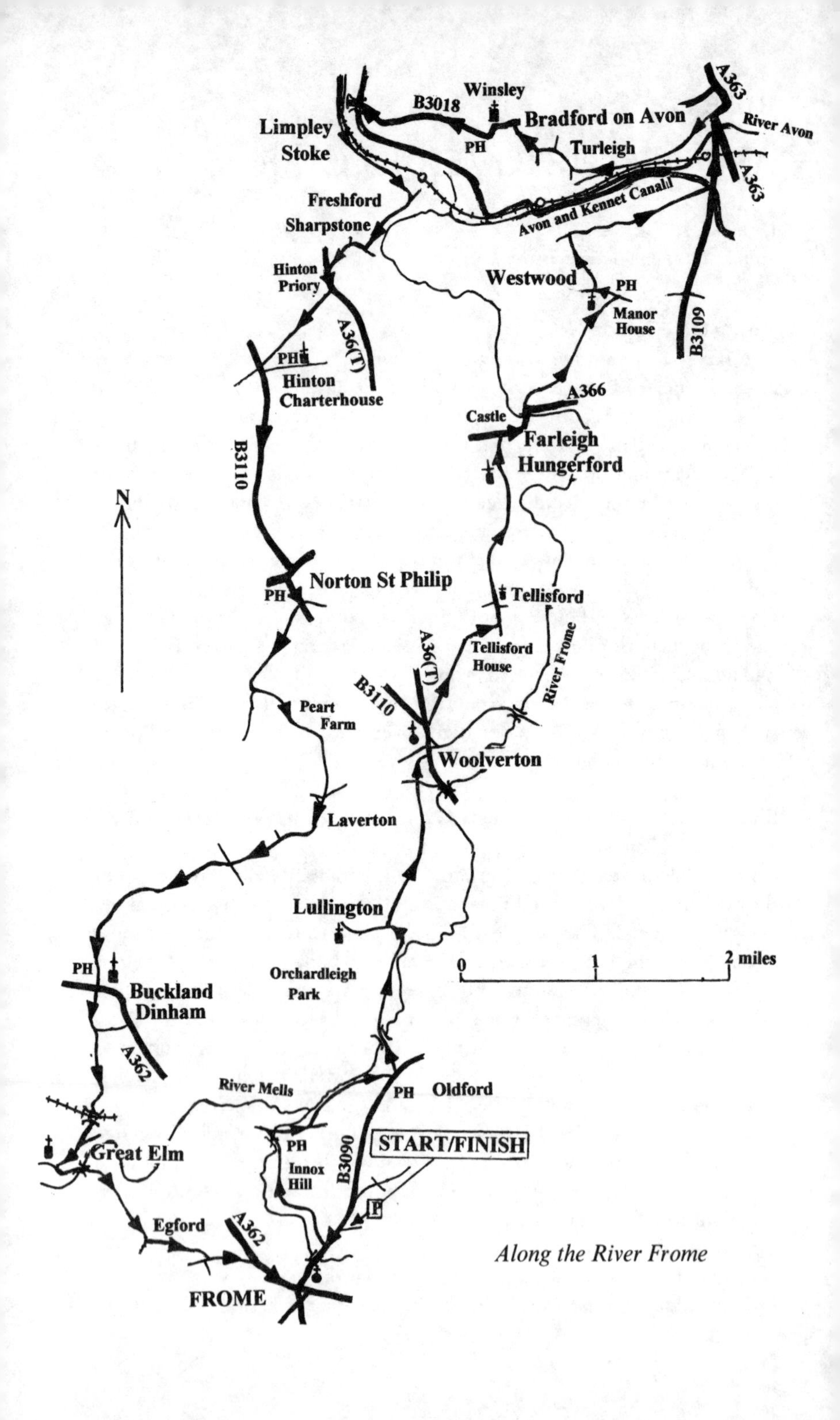

Along the River Frome

water channel running down its centre from a spring. St John's Church is of Saxon origin and Rook Lane Chapel (1707) is one of the finest in the west country.

Lullington: a picturesque village overlooking a village green with the superb church of All Saints.

Orchardleigh: a mid-19th century house in Tudor style on the site of an older building. The island church is mostly 13th century.

Stage 1 Lullington – Woolverton – Farleigh Hungerford

The road from Lullington to Woolverton is narrow but has a good surface. At the crossroads continue directly ahead to Woolverton (0.25 miles). At the A36(T) turn left and ride to a point just beyond the junction with the B3110. Take the minor road to the right along the signposted road to Tellisford (1 mile). The road rises gradually and passes Tellisford House on the right whilst away to the left stands the church. Bear right to a T-junction. Turn left and at the next crossroads ride straight on with Tellisford church away to the right. Continue to Farleigh Hungerford passing the Farleigh Hungerford church on the left before reaching the A366. Turn right and pass the entrance to Farleigh Hungerford Castle on the left. Continue down and round the sharp left-hand turn over the two river bridges. Go straight on and up the minor road to Westwood (1.75 miles). Do not follow the A366.

Points of interest

Tellisford: a pretty village with a three-arched bridge over the River Frome. The 15th century church has Norman carvings.

Farleigh Hungerford (English Heritage): the present castle stands on the site of an early manor belonging to the Montfort family until 1337, when it passed to the Hungerfords who fortified and extended it. They incorporated the parish church as a private chapel. The history of the family is a record of murder, misplaced loyalty and executions. Open all the year round to visitors.

Stage 2 Westwood – Bradford on Avon – Turleigh – Limpley Stoke – Freshford – Sharpstone

The road to Westwood rises steeply but soon flattens out and passes through pleasant farmland. In the village of Westwood, the church and Westwood Manor (NT) with its large Tythe Barn, are adjacent to one another. Continue to the T-Junction and the New Inn. Turn left and then first right. At the next T-junction turn right down a narrow lane, continue down Jones Hill to the B3109 (Frome Road) near the Kennet and Avon Canal. Turn left, cross the bridge over the canal and proceed past the Lock Inn and the Canal Tavern. Follow the B3109 to where it merges with the A363 to become St Margaret's Street. Cross over the River Avon and turn left along Market Street (the Bath Road). At the top of Market Street turn left to Turleigh (1.5 miles) along Newtown and its continuation Belcombe Road. Where the road forks bear right up the hill to Turleigh. There are excellent views down the valley from this point.

Follow the road through Turleigh and bear right up to the junction with the B3108 (Bath Road). Turn left to Limpley Stoke (1.5 miles). Continue to a sharp S-bend at Winsley passing the church on the right and the Seven Stars Inn on the left. The road then descends into the valley of the Avon down to the river and canal. Cross over the river and canal and pass under the railway bridge. Turn left immmediately and ride along Lower Stoke Road to Freshford. At the next T-junction turn left down to Freshford. Pass the village hall on the right and turn right at the signpost to Sharpstone. The road through Sharpstone is very narrow and at the T-junction opposite an archway to Abbotsleigh Stables turn right up a steep, narrow lane (Rosemary Lane) to a T-junction. Turn left to the A36(T) and Hinton Priory.

Points of interest

Bradford-on-Avon (Wilts.): delightful town with old world charm found in its narrow passages and steps, and attractive houses. Many buildings are worth exploring.

Westwood Manor (NT): partly 15th century onwards. It has Jacobean plaster ceilings and modern topiary gardens.

Stage 3 Sharpstone – Hinton Charterhouse – Norton St Philip – Buckland Dinham

Turn left at the A36(T) and take the first turn on the right to Hinton Charterhouse. This is a long straight road, and at the crossroads in the village of Hinton Charterhouse turn left onto the B3110 to Norton St Philip. On entering the village follow the S-bend past the George Inn on the right. Continue out of the village along the B3110 and take the first unsignposted turn on the right (opposite Telford Lane), which is a short distance from the centre. This minor road leads to Laverton. Follow the lane to a sharp left-hand bend and a division of roads. Bear left and continue past Peart Farm on the left. At the next crossroads take the road to Buckland Dinham (2.5 miles).

The road leads down to Laverton and then climbs to a crossroads. Cross over to the Buckland Dinham road (1.5 miles). The whole countryside in this area is pleasant rolling farmland and fairly isolated. Continue into Buckland Dinham to a crossroads with the A362 near the Bell Inn.

Points of interest

Hinton Charterhouse and Priory (Avon): founded about 1232 by the strict Carthusian Order. Much remains of the priory which is privately owned. Open to the public during the summer.

Norton St Philip: an interesting village which was once part of the estate of Hinton Charterhouse and a collecting point for Mendip wool. Samuel Pepys dined at 'The George Inn', a 14th century inn, which was also the headquarters of the Duke of Monmouth. Some of his supporters were hanged there.

Laverton: noted for its spinning wool during Frome's flourishing woollen industry; attractive manor just north of the church.

Stage 4 Buckland Dinham – Great Elm – Frome

Cross the A362 and join the narrow road to Great Elm (1 mile). Follow the winding road to Great Elm passing under a railway bridge before reaching a T-junction. Turn right into the village as far as the church and turn left down a narrow lane near a triangular piece of land. This leads to the River Mells. Cross the river, ignore the first turn on the left after the river crossing and take the next road on the left to Egford. Follow this road until it reaches a junction on the outskirts of Frome. Turn left down Egford Lane, bear left onto Broadway and at the roundabout on the A362 bear right. Continue to Bath Street, turn left and return to the car park.

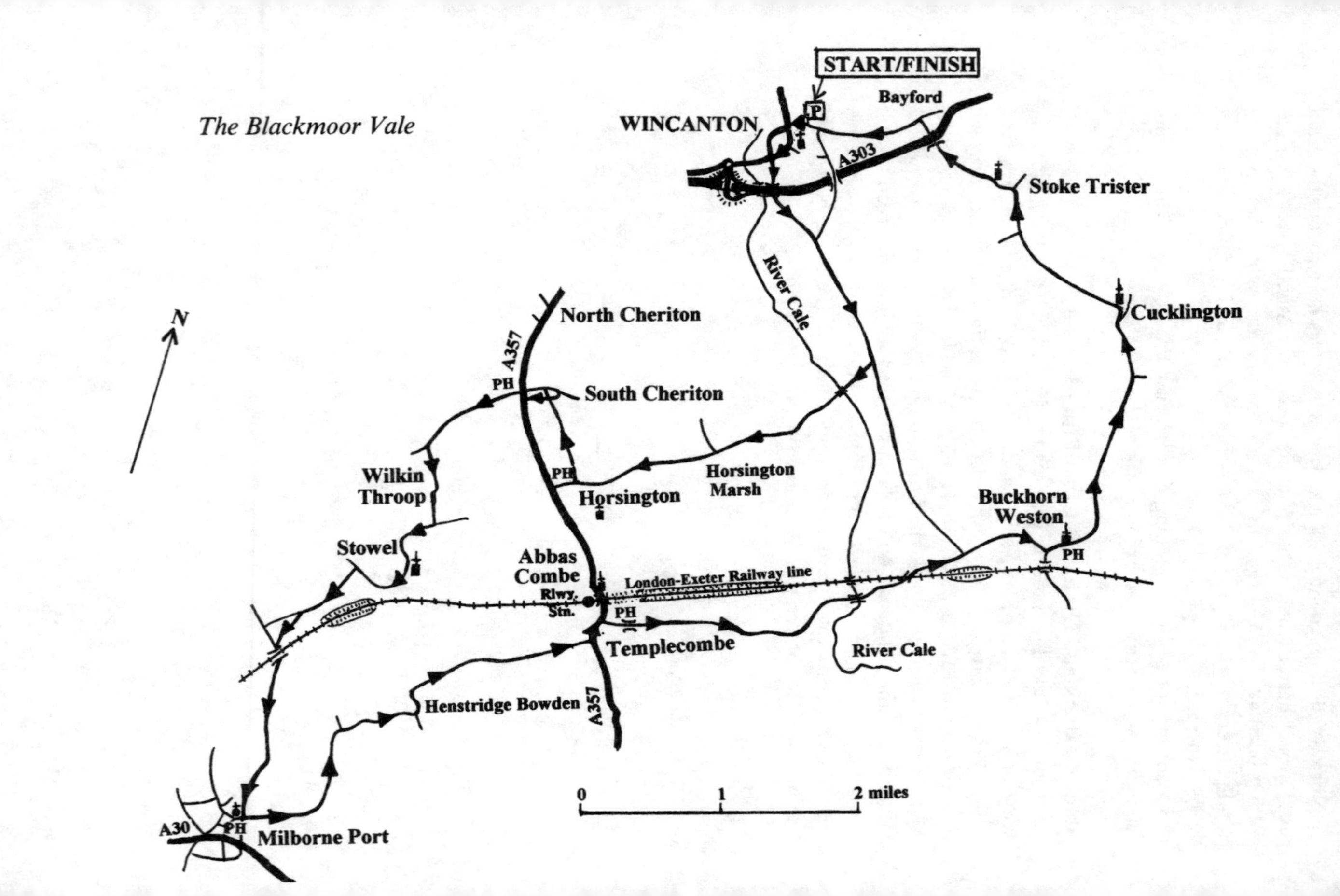
The Blackmoor Vale
START/FINISH
P
Bayford
WINCANTON
A303
Stoke Trister
River Cale
Cucklington
N
North Cheriton
A357
PH
South Cheriton
Wilkin
Throop
PH
Horsington
Horsington
Marsh
Buckhorn
Weston
PH
Stowel
Abbas
Combe
Rlwy.
Stn.
London-Exeter Railway line
PH
Templecombe
River Cale
Henstridge Bowden
A357
0
1
2 miles
A30
PH
Milborne Port

RIDE 5

THE BLACKMOOR VALE

Distance: Short route: 23.5 miles.
Journey time: approximately 4-5 hours.
Extended route: 26 miles.
Journey time: approximately 5-6 hours.

Route Description:
Wincanton lies at the head of the Blackmoor Vale, a flat valley which was formerly wooded and part of Selwood Forest. Its beauty was an inspiration to Thomas Hardy when writing *Tess of the D'Urbervilles.* Its pastoral charm gives it a unique character, but sadly this southern part of Somerset along the Dorset border does not feature prominently in the publicised attractions of the county.

Any tour that starts off downhill is bound to give confidence, particularly if it is followed by a good distance along the flat. From Wincanton the road drops to the level plain of the valley and winds its way through the delightful villages of Horsington and South Cheriton, rising gently to Wilkin Throop before dropping down to Stowell and Milborne Port. A climb is necessary to reach Henstridge Bowden from Milborne Port but the wonderful views are a fine reward.

Templecombe offers refreshments at the Royal Wessex public house which also holds the key to the door of St Mary's Church. In the church there is a painting on a wooden panel, dated 1280, that is believed to be a copy of the figure on the Turin Holy Shroud. The tour continues by crossing the valley once more, passing briefly into the Dorset village of Buckhorn Weston before climbing the ridge to Cucklington, Stoke Trister and back to Wincanton. Anyone wishing to shorten the tour may do so on the Templecombe to Buckhorn Weston road by turning left just beyond the bridge over the main railway line.

Start: (O.S. Landranger sheet 183, Grid reference ST712287)
Leave the car park in Carrington Way, Wincanton, and turn right down the main street past the White Horse Hotel. Bear left down the one-way street past the Plaza Cinema to a signposted junction. Turn left towards Buckhorn Weston passing under the A303. The road is flat, and winds along the bottom of the valley. At the first junction on the right (2.3 miles) follow the signposted road to Horsington (2.5 miles). The road eventually crosses a bridge over a disused railway track before entering Horsington, with its handsome stone-built houses and village pond.

Stage 1 Over the rim of the valley from Horsington to Milborne Port

Before reaching the Half Moon Inn in Horsington, take the first turn on the right passing the village hall and the Primary School on the outskirts of the village. Pass the cemetery outside South Cheriton and follow the road round to the left to the A357. To see the village turn right and at the White Hart Inn turn right again into South Cheriton. Follow the road downhill into this most attractive village passing the smithy on the left. Bear round to the right, and right again by a fieldgate thus completing the looping tour and return to the A357. Turn right here and then left towards Stowel at the White Hart Inn. The narrow lane winds up through the hamlet of Wilkin Throop to a T-junction. There is no signpost here, but to the left down the road there is a large house with a clocktower in the grounds. Turn right at this junction passing Wilkin Throop House on the right. Follow the left-hand bend from where there are wonderful views over the surrounding countryside. Continue down this looping road past the church of St Mary Magdalene on the left and into the hamlet of Stowel. Turn sharp left just beyond the telephone box and along to a sign which indicates 2.5 miles to Milborne Port. At the fork bear left to a junction. Turn left here, pass under a railway bridge, past a church with a small spire on the right, to the Give Way sign in North Street. This is the junction with the A30. Refreshments can be obtained from the Queen's Head Hotel nearby.

Points of interest

South Cheriton: a delightful village with houses and cottages of all ages. The pleasure of the tour would be diminished if the village was not visited.

Wilkin Throop: not mentioned in guide books but a gem nevertheless.

Stage 2 From the rim of the Blackmoor Vale at Templecombe across the valley to Cucklington and Wincanton

From Milborne Port return along North Street to the church with the small spire. At this point turn right into Wheathill Lane. Follow this lane past Wheathill Lane Nurseries on the right and climb the steep tree-lined hillside. At the top the narrow road runs along the edge of a steep escarpment to the left with Spurles Farm on the right. There are superb views from the ridge. The road drops down from the ridge before climbing up through Henstridge Bowden to a signpost. Turn left to Templecombe (1.5 miles).

At the A357 turn left. Take the first turn on the right at a triangle of grass and ride over a disused railway bridge onto the flat farmland of the Blackmoor Vale. Continue along this winding road over the River Cale, and then over the main railway line. At a distance of 0.25 miles from this bridge there is a junction to the left which leads directly to Wincanton. Anyone wishing to return at this point should take this road. Those wishing to continue should carry straight on to Buckhorn Weston. At the T-junction in the centre of the village turn left up Church Hill passing the Post Office and the church on the left, with the Stapleton Arms on the right. Climb to the summit of the ridge and at the next fork (no signpost here) bear left along Shave Hill to Cucklington. Continue along this road passing tall stone gate posts on the left just before the village. Follow the signposted road to Stoke Trister which dips past a row of cottages to a superb viewpoint. Continue down the hill past the church on the right, along the valley and straight up and through Stoke Trister. At a fork in the village bear left with the church on the right. Continue under the A303 to Bayford on the outskirts of Wincanton and from there return to the starting point in the centre of the town.

Points of interest

Templecombe: comprises two parts, Abbas Combe and Temple Combe, which derived its name from the Knights Templar who had a chapel there founded in the 12th century. The railway station is worth a visit to see the station and its unusual sculptures.

Buckhorn Weston: a pleasant Dorset village standing beneath the east rim of Blackmoor Vale.

Bruton Forest and King Alfred's Tower

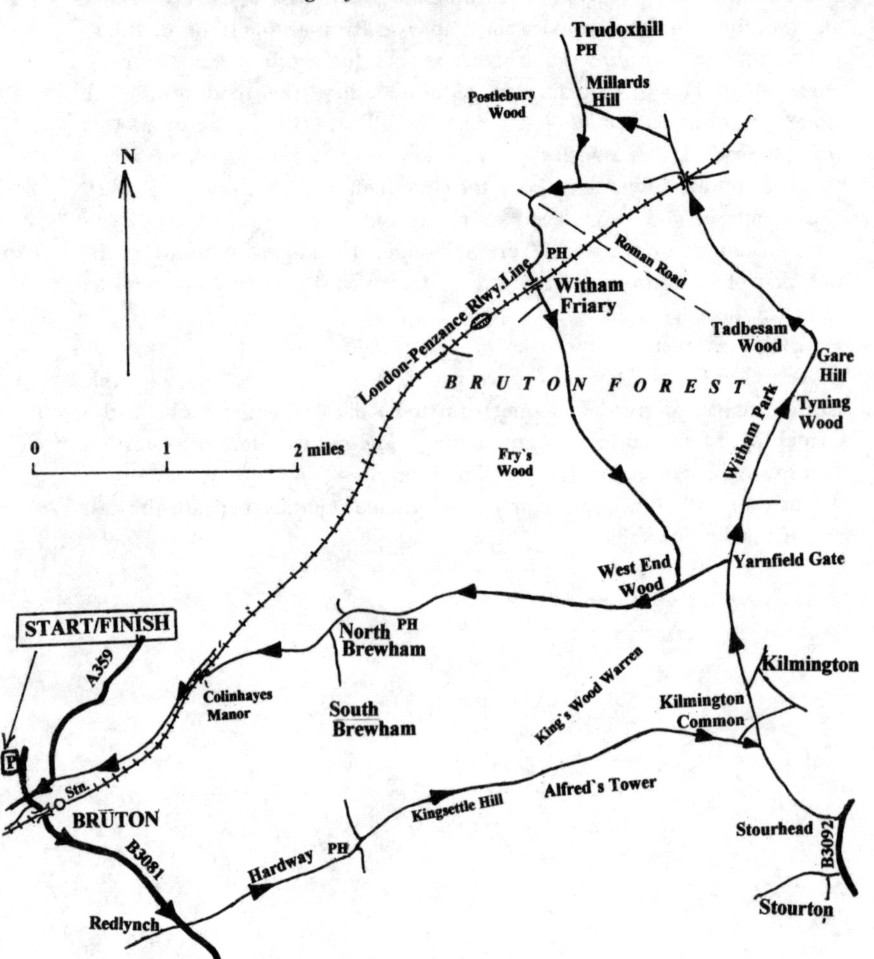

RIDE 6

BRUTON FOREST AND ALFRED'S TOWER

Distance: Short route: 14.5 miles.
Journey time: approximately 3-4 hours.
Extended route: 31 miles.
Journey time: approximately 6 hours.
(These distances and times do not include the 3.5 miles from Kilmington Common to Stourhead and return or the length of stay.)

Route Description

Bruton Forest is today a collection of woods concentrated in an area to the south of Frome and to the east of Bruton. The whole of this area is part of the once large forest of Selwood, which stretched from near Bath down to Dorset. It included all the land eastwards to the Wiltshire chalklands and in places marked the boundary between Somerset and Wiltshire. The present patchwork of woods is the result of the gradual deforestation and conversion to agriculture begun by the Saxons and expanded as the demand for wood grew under the Tudors. It is an appropriate setting for a memorial to King Alfred.

Two routes are offered, each of different length, but each providing the cyclist with an appreciation of an area of Somerset which has seen dramatic changes. On both routes there are two major climbs. The first is from Bruton to Redlynch, and the second the short but steep climb up Kingsettle Hill. For those who choose the extended route there is a further short but steep climb up through the West End Wood to the junction with the Yarnfield to North Brewham road. On both routes there are long compensatory rides downhill.

Start for both the long and short routes: (O.S. Landranger sheet 183, Grid reference ST683346)

From the car park in Coombe Street (B3081) Bruton, turn right and follow the road down to the church. Bear left (the River Brue on the left), pass under the railway bridge and climb for 1.4 miles up to the crossroads at Redlynch. Turn left and follow the Hardway downhill past the Bull Inn on the left and straight on. Turn right at the next junction. Climb up Kingsettle Hill passing Hillcombe Farm on the way to King Alfred's Tower at the summit. From Alfred's Tower continue to the Give-Way sign at Kilmington Common. Those who wish to visit Stourhead should turn right at this junction and continue to the B3092.

Turn right to Stourton (approx. 0.5 miles) where a signposted road leads to Stourhead House and Gardens (National Trust). To return to Kilmington Common turn left at the B3092 and then first left back to the junction at Kilmington Common.

From this junction continue to Yarnfield Gate, passing the village of Kilmington away on the right. At Yarnfield Gate those taking the shorter route turn left at this junction. Those taking the extended route bear right with Witham Park on the left.

Description of the short route from Yarnfield Gate to North Brewham and Bruton. From Yarnfield Gate follow the road, flanked by West End Wood and King's Wood Warren, downhill in a stepped progression. Pass the Old Red Lion Inn in North Brewham and Colinhayes Manor on the left before passing under the railway line. Bear left back to Bruton.

Description of the extended route from Yarnfield Gate to Trudoxhill, Witham Friary and back to the junction with Yarnfield Gate and from there to North Brewham and Bruton. From Yarnfield Gate bear right, with Witham Park on the left. At the fork take the road to Frome with Witham Park on the left and Tyning Wood on the right. The road bears left and downhill at Gare Hill with Tadbesam Wood on the left. There are wonderful views from here towards Frome and Trudoxhill. Pass over the railway bridge, ignore the road on the left to Witham Friary and carry straight on. At the next junction bear left past Iron Mill Farm and up Millards Hill to a junction near Postlebury Wood. The village of Trudoxhill is 0.75 miles away and refreshments can be obtained from the White Hart Inn.

Return to the junction near Postlebury Wood and bear right to Witham Friary 2 miles away. From here the the road climbs steadily before running down to a very sharp left-hand bend. Take care at this bend. Continue through Witham Friary, past the church and the Seymour Arms and under the railway bridge. At the signpost outside the village carry straight on towards Kilmington. The road is flat at this point, with Fry's Wood to the right and Alfred's Tower ahead. Climb up through the West End Wood to join the road from Yarnfield to North Brewham and Bruton. Please see the details for this final section in the short route description.

Points of interest

Bruton: Sexey's Hospital (1638) and the former Abbey Court House, King's School (endowed 1519), Bow Bridge over the River Brue, dovecote of the old abbey buildings, the Blue Ball Hotel with its Georgian Assembly Rooms, St Mary's Church.

Witham Friary: early site of the first Carthusian monastery, founded by Henry II as an act of penance after the murder of Thomas a' Becket.

King Alfred's Tower: built in 1772 to commemorate the place where King Alfred raised his standard against the Danes in 878. 160 feet high, it is in the care of the National Trust and is open to the public from April to October.

Kingsettle Hill: the site of an early trackway, 'The Harrow Way', which linked the hill forts of the area and continued down through Hardway to Halstock, south-west of Yeovil.

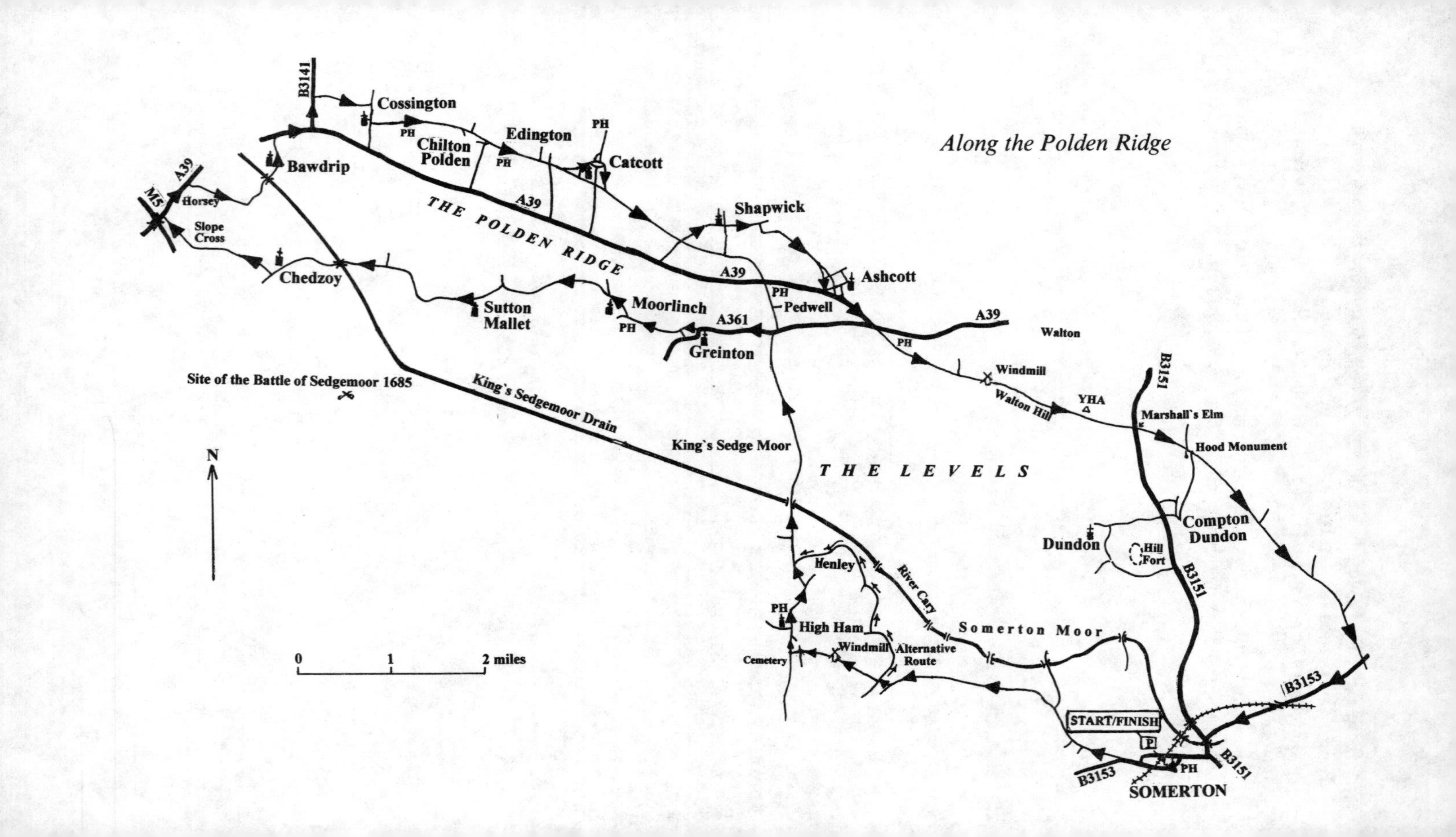
Along the Polden Ridge
B3141
Cossington
Chilton
Polden
Edington
PH
Catcott
Bawdrip
A39
M5
Horsey
Slope
Cross
THE POLDEN RIDGE
Shapwick
Chedzoy
Sutton
Mallet
Moorlinch
Ashcott
Pedwell
A361
Greinton
Walton
Windmill
Walton Hill
YHA
Site of the Battle of Sedgemoor 1685
King's Sedgemoor Drain
King's Sedge Moor
THE LEVELS
B3151
Marshall's Elm
Hood Monument
Compton
Dundon
Dundon
Hill
Fort
Henley
River Cary
High Ham
Cemetery
Alternative
Route
Somerton Moor
START/FINISH
P
B3153
SOMERTON
N
0
1
2 miles

RIDE 7

ALONG THE POLDEN RIDGE

Distance: 36 miles returning via Compton Dundon.
Journey time: approximately 6 hours.
Distance: 38 miles returning via the Hood Monument.)
Journey time: approximately 6½ hours.

Route Description

The Polden Hills rise from the flatlands of the Somerset Levels in the form of a thin ridge which separates the moors of Avelon and the Mendips to the north, and Sedgemoor and the high plateau of High Ham to the south. Villages lie on both slopes, separated by the course of a Roman road, now the A39. This journey begins in Somerton and runs across Somerton Moor, over High Ham, down onto King's Sedge Moor, and then through the villages on the southern and northern slopes of the Poldens before returning to Somerton.

The route is made for easy riding with few hills. Those of significance include that from Somerton Moor to High Ham, the hill leading to Walton Hill and the two from Compton Dundon to Somerton. The reward for the climb to High Ham, be it on foot or bicycle, is a visit to the Somerset landmark of Stembridge Tower Mill (National Trust) and the panoramic views of the surrounding countryside. If this climb is too daunting, an alternative route is offered around the base of High Ham to Henley before continuing the journey (see the small arrowed section on the map).

The route offers the beauty of the flatlands, charming villages, expansive views and the company of the ghosts of the Romans, Cromwell's army, the Duke of Monmouth and the Battle of Sedgemoor, King Alfred and King Arthur. With such a combination of the past and present the tour excites the imagination and maintains a high of level interest and pleasure.

Start: (O.S. Landranger sheets 182 and 193, Grid reference for sheet 193 ST487284)

Turn right at the entrance to the car park off West Street in Somerton. Continue along the B3153 (West Street) towards Langport. After 0.5 miles take a right fork signposted Low Ham and Westcombe. The road passes an industrial estate on the right before dipping down to the flat area of Somerton Moor with the River Cary on the right. Continue to a signpost near a bungalow. Turn right to Low Ham and the next junction approximately 100 yards ahead, take the unmarked road directly ahead to High Ham. This road gently rises but gradually becomes steeper. At the top there is the

Eastfield Nature Reserve on the right and the Stembridge Tower Mill ahead to the left. (For the less hilly alternative route to Henley please see the small arrowed route on the map).

From the top of the hill continue to a T-junction opposite the cemetery. Turn right to the village, passing the church on the left, to a viewing point on the right about halfway through the village. Pass the King's Head public house and at the fork take the road to Pedwell, a steep winding road down onto King's Sedge Moor. Care must be taken on this hill.

Points of interest

Somerton: once a royal Saxon town standing high above the Sedgemoor Levels. St Michael's and All Angels Church has a fine carved timbered roof (circa 1510) and a Jacobean pulpit dated 1615. The Market Cross and Town Hall date from the 17th century. Somerton castle and the prison built from its ruins were sited where the Globe Inn and the White Hart Inn now stand.

High Ham: Stembridge Tower Mill (NT), and the 15th century church with a fine 500 year old screen.

Stage 1 Across the moors to the villages on the southern slopes of the Poldens

Cross the moor to the A361 at Pedwell, the Taunton/Street road, and turn left to Greinton. At the church on the left, near a sharp left hand bend, look for the signpost to Moorlinch on the right-hand side of the road. In Moorlinch pass the public house and bear right up the hill to a fork in the road, which is recognised by the gated garden commemorating the coronation of Queen Elizabeth II. Bear left to Sutton Mallet passing Firsland Farm on the left, and at the next T-junction turn left to the village. The road bypasses the centre of the village but it is well worthwhile visiting the church which is quite unique. It can be reached by bearing left at the signpost to Chedzoy. On leaving the church rejoin the Chedzoy road which winds across West Moor and over the King's Sedgemoor Drain, a wide drainage channel, to Chedzoy 1.25 miles away. In Chedzoy take time to visit the church where details of the trails to the site of the Battle of Sedgemoor are on an information board.

Leave the church and pass through the village. Take the first road on the right which leads to Bridgwater. It passes through a small estate of houses and leads to the A39. Turn right away from the M5, and continue to a signpost indicating Bawdrip.

Points of interest

Moorlinch: provides magnificent views over the Levels.

Sutton Malett: unusual church with boxed pews.

Chedzoy: originally belonged to the monks of Glastonbury. It is said that the Duke of Monmouth first sighted the Royalist army from the church tower. Marks on the stone buttresses are said to have been made by the peasants when sharpening their weapons.

Bawdrip: overlooks the Levels. Of particular interest are the 13th century church and 16th century Tudor Court.

Stage 2 Along the Broadway to the villages on the northern slopes of the Poldens

Turn right off the A39 and cycle over King's Sedgemoor Drain into Bawdrip. Take the right fork in the village, passing the church on the left and continuing under the railway bridge to the A39.Turn right and then first left to Woolavington along the B3141. Continue up the hill and turn right for Cossington. Pass the church on the right and take the left-hand road to Chilton Polden.

The Red Tile Inn is 0.25 miles ahead. The road linking the villages on the northern slopes is called The Broadway and runs roughly parallel to the A39 at some distance from it. It acts as a bypass to the villages and diversions must be taken from it in order to explore Eddington, Catcott and Shapwick. Signposts clearly indicate the road to each village. This means returning to The Broadway after each visit but does not add greatly to the journey. The Broadway passes directly through Chilton Polden past the White Hart Inn and continues towards Shapwick. The diversion into Shapwick takes the rider by the church on the left. On leaving the village follow this road directly across the crossroads to the minor road leading to Ashcott. Continue along this road, take the first turn on the right passing into and through the village to rejoin the A39. Turn left and follow the A39 until it joins the A361 near the Pipers Inn. Take the minor road to the right of the inn which rises to the top of Walton Hill, passing a white windmill tower on the right. There are excellent views from here across Somerton Moor, High Ham and Compton Dundon.

Points of interest

Cossington: delightful village on the west side of the Poldens. The 'Preaching Tree' under which John Wesley is said to have preached is now a stump surrounded by concrete and decorated with heathers.

Catcott: a maze of winding lanes with attractive cottages. The 13th century church has sliding seats in the aisle for the use of servants.

Shapwick: a resting place for pilgrims journeying to and from Glastonbury Abbey. There are two manor houses, one moated, two icehouses and two dovecotes.

Stage 3 Return to Somerton

Continue along this road past the Street Youth Hostel on the left to the B3151 at Marshall's Elm. One of two routes can now be taken on this final stage of the tour.(a) Turn right and continue to Somerton along the B3151 through Compton Dundon before joining the B3153 into Somerton, or (b) cross directly over the crossroads and follow this road past the Hood Monument until it meets the B3153. Turn right and continue down the hill, under the skew railway bridge to the B3151. Turn left and after approximately 200 yards turn right to Somerton.

Points of interest

The Hood Monument: the monument honours Vice-Admiral Sir Samuel Hood, a contemporary of Lord Nelson, and a member of a family of distinguished sailors. It stands as a prominent landmark on the ridge above the village of Compton Dundon, whose 13th century church and Iron Age fort are worth a visit.

RIDE 8

ACROSS THE PEATLANDS

Distance: 23.5 miles.
Journey time: approximately 3 hours easy riding.

Route Description

It is appropriate that Glastonbury should be the starting point of a tour that journeys across the flat landscape of the Levels. Time has not removed all evidence of how the area must have appeared before the network of drainage ditches (or rhynes) were dug or the manner in which the early settlers lived. The whole of this area was flooded around 4000 BC due to the melting of the polar cap and the subsequent rise in the sea level. As the sea retreated, sedge and reeds began to grow in the drying mud. Later climatic conditions encouraged the growth of cotton grass, heathers, moss and the subsquent swampy conditions. Areas of raised bog above the surface were known as islands and were inhabited by early man. Godney was one of these so-called Lake villages, and prospered about 250 BC. At Bleadney the road rises gradually from the Levels onto a long low 'island' where the village of Wedmore stands dominant. From Wedmore the route returns to the Levels and winds its way across the moor over the River Brue to an area of commercial peat extraction between Burtle and Westhay. The final stage of the journey through the village of Meare provides further clues to the nature of the area prior to the drainage of the Levels. The first is the name Meare, about which the Domesday Book mentions '10 fishermen and 3 fisheries on this island'. The other clues include the manor house near the church and the Abbot's Fish House, which formerly stood near a large pool.

Start: (O.S.Landranger sheet 182, Grid reference ST496396)

From the car park in St John's Street, Glastonbury, turn right into Northload Street and follow the B3151 out of town, over a bridge, and onto the moor. Take the first road (signposted) on the right to Godney and at a fork bear left. At the apex of this fork, in a field to the right, can be seen the faint trace of hillocks, the site of a Lake village. Continue along this straight road, round an elongated S-bend and over Decoy Rhyne bridge before entering the village of Godney.

Points of interest

Glastonbury: a place of pilgrimage wrapped in history, mystery and legend. The site of the earliest foundations of English Christianity. The Tor towers above the town and is a landmark for miles around. Places to visit

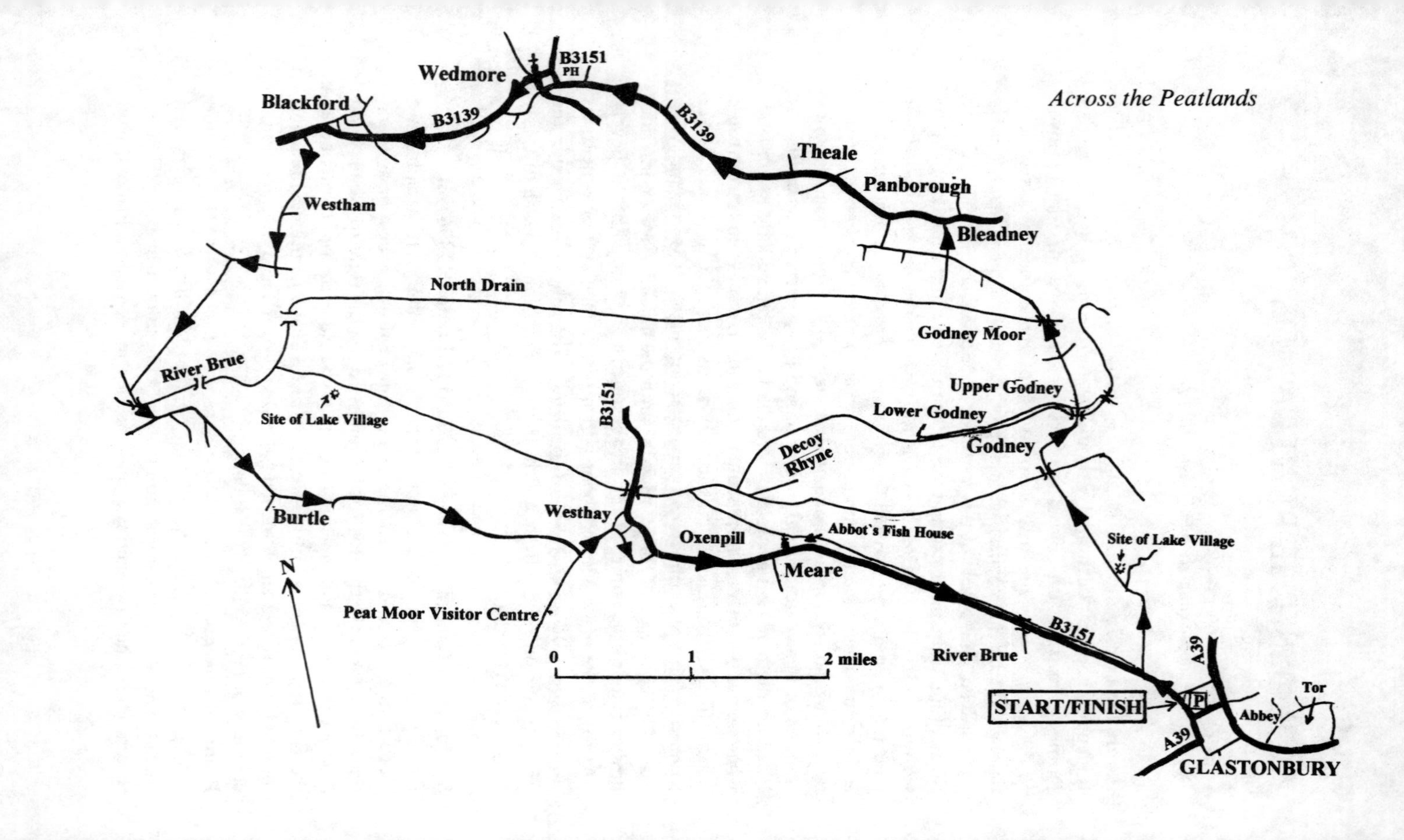
Wedmore
B3151
PH
Blackford
B3139
B3139
Theale
Panborough
Bleadney
Westham
North Drain
Godney Moor
River Brue
Upper Godney
Lower Godney
Site of Lake Village
B3151
Godney
Decoy Rhyne
Burtle
Westhay
Oxenpill
Abbot's Fish House
Site of Lake Village
Meare
N
Peat Moor Visitor Centre
B3151
River Brue
0
1
2 miles
A39
Tor
START/FINISH
P
Abbey
A39
GLASTONBURY

include the Abbey, the Tribunal (which now serves as a museum), Tor Hill, the Abbey Barn Rural Life Museum and the George and Pilgrim Hotel, an old pilgrim hostelry.

Stage 1 Godney to Wedmore

From the Stop sign at the crossroads just beyond the bridge in Godney, cross directly to join the road to Panborough and Wedmore (5.25 miles ahead). At the next crossroads, marked Fenny Castle to the right and Westhay to the left, carry straight on. Cross a bridge over the North Drain and ride along a further stretch of straight road before bearing left to an unsignposted crossroads. Turn right to the B3139 at Bleadney and then left for Wedmore (3.5 miles ahead). The Mendip Hills can be seen to the right. Continue through Panborough and up past the Panborough Inn on the right and on into Theale. On the outskirts of Wedmore the Church of St Mary can be seen directly ahead. At the Give Way sign turn right into The Borough, part of the B3151 road to Cheddar. Refreshments can be obtained from the Swan Inn opposite Church Street.

Points of interest

Godney: associated with the legend of King Arthur and the site of an Iron Age Lake Village. Details of the archeological finds are to be seen in the Glastonbury museum.

Wedmore: an island in ancient times and site of the peace treaty between King Alfred and the Dane, Guthrum, in 878. It is an attractive village formed around an open green and includes the Porch House (17th century) and two Italian style buildings in Church Street. The church has a fine Jacobean pulpit, a mural of St Christopher and a window commemorating the Jubilee of Queen Victoria.

Stage 2 Wedmore – Blackford – Burtle – Westhay – Meare – Glastonbury

Leave Wedmore by taking the road up Church Street past the George Hotel and the Church of St Mary. Continue along the B3139 towards Burnham, passing the Wedmore Sports Ground on the right. Take the first left turn signposted to Westham, just beyond the sharp left hand bend at Blackford. Beyond Westham the route returns to the Levels, and Glastonbury Tor can be seen in the distance.

Take the first turn on the right after Westham and at the next junction turn left towards Edington. After aproximately 1.25 miles turn left at the T-junction, cross a humpbacked bridge over the River Brue to another junction. Turn left towards Edington and round a right hand bend into Burtle. Pass through the village in the direction of Glastonbury. Between Burtle and Westhay peat has been extracted and stored in large mounds, causing the road to stand higher than the peat beds. Turn right at the next junction to visit the Peat Moors Visitors Centre, and the reconstruction of an Iron Age settlement, and ancient wooden trackways that crossed this area.

To return to Westhay retrace the journey to the junction. Continue through the village and at the B3151 turn right to Meare. Continue through Meare passing the manor house and Abbot's Fish House on the left before returning to Glastonbury alongside the River Brue.

Points of interest

Westhay: Peat Moors Visitors Centre at 'The Willows' Garden Centre.

Meare: remains of a Lake village, 14th century Abbot's Fish House, the Manor built as a retreat for the Abbots of Glastonbury.

RIDE 9

ALLER, ATHELNEY AND KING ALFRED

Distance: 23 miles.
Journey time: approximately 4 hours.

Route Description
The journey begins with a steep climb from Langport to a high point above the surrounding moors, before descending to Aller where Guthrum the leader of the Danes, was converted to Christianity following his defeat by King Alfred in 878. Furthermore, Burrow Mump, the Isle of Athelney and East Lyng form a trio of prominent mounds of land that interrupt the flat surrounding landscape and which served the King as observation point, refuge and a defensive system respectively.

The journey from West Lyng entails a ride across the moors to the higher ground at North Curryand from there along the ridge to Meare Green and Stoke St Gregory before returning to the moors at Stathe, the final stage before Langport. Apart from the initial climb up the hill in Langport the remainder of the route makes for an easy and interesting ride.

Start: (O.S. Landranger sheets 182 and 193, Grid reference for sheet 193 ST417266)
From the exit of the precinct car park in Langport turn right into the main street (A378) past the Langport Arms Hotel and continue up the steep hill directly ahead. At the top the road sweeps the left past the church, through the archway of the Hanging Chapel and downhill to Huish Episcopi church on the left at the A372. Turn left towards Bridgwater passing over the railway to the B3153. Take the road directly opposite to Wearne. The final part of this road bears sharply to the right and uphill to join the main road through Wearne. Turn immediately left and continue out of the village to the A372.
Points of interest
Langport: once a thriving port built on an artificial causeway to the River Parrett. The oldest part of Langport is The Hill with its 14th century Hanging Chapel. In July 1645 Cromwell's army routed the Royalist forces at the Battle of Langport, the last battle of the Civil War.

Stage 1 Wearne – Aller – Burrowbridge – Athelney – East Lyng
Turn right onto the A372 and follow the road into Aller. Turn left at the

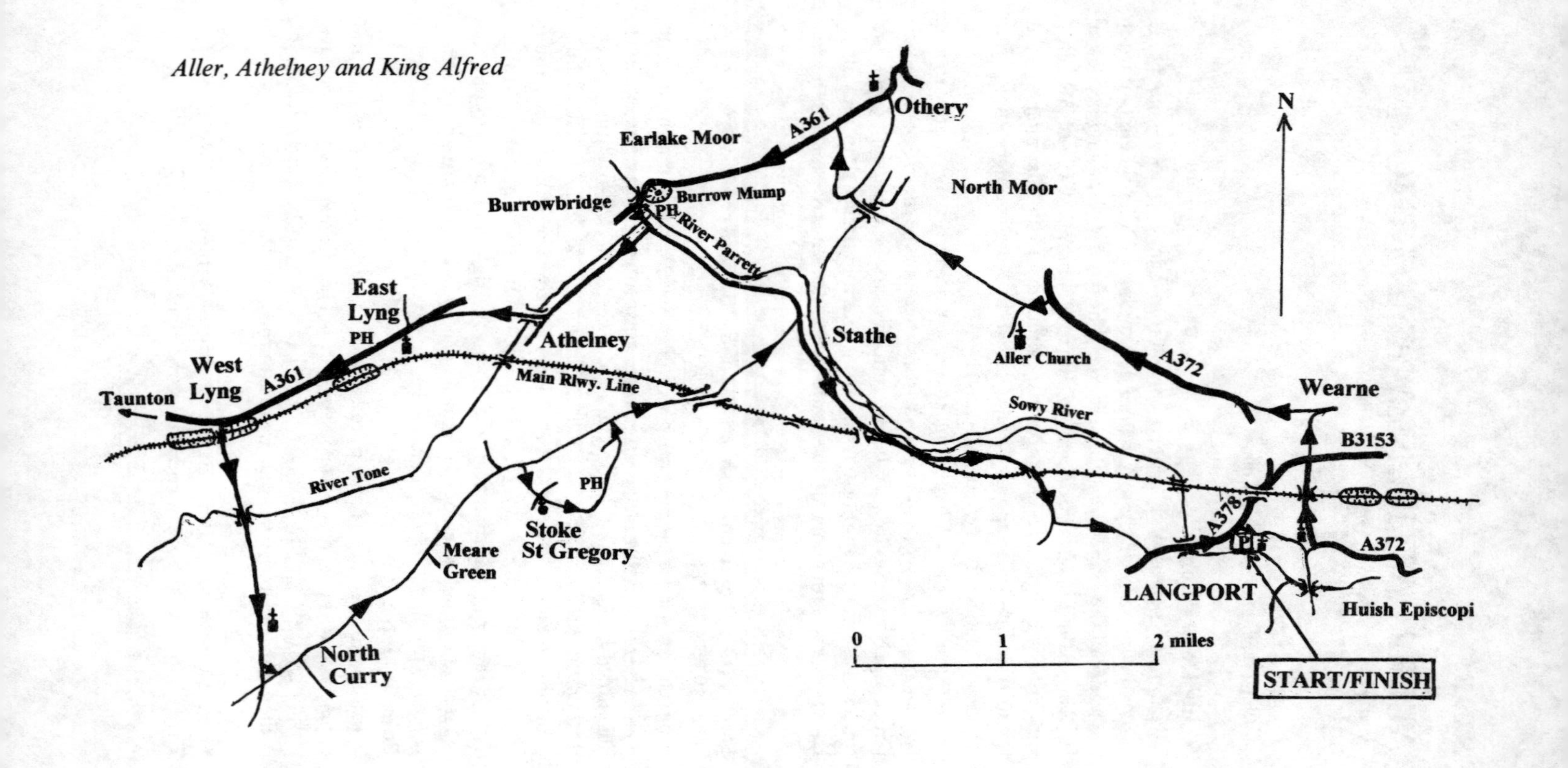
Aller, Athelney and King Alfred
Othery
N
A361
Earlake Moor
North Moor
Burrow Mump
Burrowbridge
PH
River Parrett
East
Lyng
PH
Athelney
Stathe
Aller Church
A372
West
Lyng
A361
Main Rlwy. Line
Wearne
Taunton
Sowy River
B3153
River Tone
PH
A378
Stoke
St Gregory
A372
Meare
Green
LANGPORT
Huish Episcopi
0
1
2 miles
North
Curry
START/FINISH

Pound Inn and where the road bears sharply to the right take the minor road to the left leading to the 12th century church.

Follow the road across the moor, with Burrow Mump clearly visible to the left. Pass over the small river bridge and at the T-junction turn left. The road swings round a right-hand bend past the Pathe Barn on the left and uphill to the A361. Turn left to a summit near the cemetery before running down steeply to the moors. The road runs in a straight line along a raised causeway to Burrow Mump, a prominent and natural mound with the remains of a church on the summit. A climb to the top is well rewarded by the magnificent views.

From Burrow Mump ride into the village of Burrowbridge past the King Alfred Inn. Cross the bridge over the River Parrett and take the first turn on the left towards Athelney. Cross over the River Tone and take the signposted right turn along Stanmore Road to Athelney. Turn right at the signpost to Lyng and cross the River Tone again. To the right a small obelisk to King Alfred stands on high ground behind farm buildings. This high ground was the Isle of Athelney. Continue to the A361 and notice how the final section of this road runs along what appears to be a raised causeway, which may be a remnant of Alfred's defensive system linking East Lyng and Athelney. Turn left onto the A361 and pass through East Lyng with the Rose and Crown on the right.

Points of interest

Aller: famous for its association with King Alfred, who had Guthrum the Danish leader baptised and converted to Christianity on the site of the church.

Athelney: the island winter refuge of King Alfred the Great in 877-878 and where he planned his offensive strategy against the invading Danes, and where he subsequently built an Abbey to commemorate his victory over Guthrum. The Abbey existed until 1539 and although no traces remain above ground an obelisk marks its site.

Burrow Mump (NT): site of an ancient hill fort and possibly used by King Alfred as an observation point over the moors. It was bought to commemorate the dead of the First World War. The chapel at the top dates from the 19th century.

Burrowbridge: once a river port and place where the Rivers Parrett and Tone meet.

East Lyng: the fortified island at the end of the causeway which linked it to the Island of Athelney and where Alfred built his fort and defensive ditches. The fort is located in the orchard near the church in the village. Today the road to the A361 follows part of this causeway (see route details).

Stage 2 East Lyng – West Lyng – North Curry – Stoke St Gregory – Stathe – Langport

Continue along the A361 and take the turn on the left signposted 'the Willows and Wetlands Craft Trail', North Curry (1.75 miles) and Stoke St Gregory (3.25 miles). The road crosses over the main railway line, continues across the moors, over the River Tone, with North Curry church ahead standing high above the moors. The road leads to the War Memorial in the centre of the village. Bear left by the Memorial and left again down Stoke Road. Travel along the ridge of high ground which stretches from North Curry to Stathe, passing through Mere Green to the Willows and Wetlands Visitor Centre. Where the road turns left to Athelney keep straight ahead to Stoke St Gregory. Turn right into the village and at the junction with Huntham Road keep straight on with the church to the right. Keep bearing to the left. This passes the Rose and Crown Inn and round a large S-bend to a T-junction. Turn right to Stathe. Cross the bridge over the main railway line and at the T-junction in Stathe turn right. At the fork near the railway bridge keep left and follow the signposted road to the A378. Turn left, pass over the River Parrett and along the main road to the precinct car park.

Points of interest

North Curry: a delightful village and a royal manor until the 14th century. It has been the centre of the willow industry for centuries. The 14th century church is known as the 'Cathedral of the Moors' and the churchyard contains a Saxon Cross said to have come from Alfred's Abbey at Athelney.

Stoke St Gregory: is part of the 'Withy Trail' and a basket-making centre.

RIDE 10

A RIDE ROUND GLASTONBURY TOR

Distance: 33 miles.
Journey time: approximately 5-6 hours.

Route Description
On this ride Glastonbury Tor is seldom out of sight, and serves as the focal point of a journey that begins in Street and climbs its way steadily to Butleigh and Kingweston, where there are expansive views over a beautiful landscape. Keinton Mandeville is barely touched as the route turns north to Barton St. David, where a visit to the church with its American connections is rewarding.

The journey continues to Baltonsborough and Southtown, a small hamlet near West Pennard. The climb to Southtown is up Pennard Hill along a narrow lane of increasing steepness. At the top, the absence of signposts requires careful reading of the guide notes or of the Landranger map in order to find and enjoy the pleasure of the ride down Stickleball Hill to the A361. Care should be taken in the descent, particularly in wet conditions.

From the A361 the road passes North Wootton, Launcherley and Woodford on its journey to Wells from where a return is made to the Levels. The route through Castle, Polsham and Godney provides a real 'taste' of the moorland scene. The final stretch of the journey completes the circle with a last look at the Tor before returning to Street.

Apart from the climb up Pennard Hill the ride is well within the capability of the average rider. The journey around the Tor provides panoramic views, contrasting scenery, pleasant villages and the opportunity to explore the historic city of Wells.

Start: (O.S. Landranger sheet 182, Grid reference ST482366)
Leave the central car park in Street and turn right. At the junction with the High Street turn left passing the Shoe Museum on the left and the Bear Hotel on the right. At the mini-roundabout turn right along the B3151 (Somerton Road) passing the Street Inn on the left. Climb uphill to the traffic lights, turn left and follow the road past Millfield School on the right. The road bears round to the right passing the Millfield sports fields and winds its way to a signpost to Glastonbury. Keep straight on through Butleigh Wootton to Butleigh.

A Ride round Glastonbury Tor

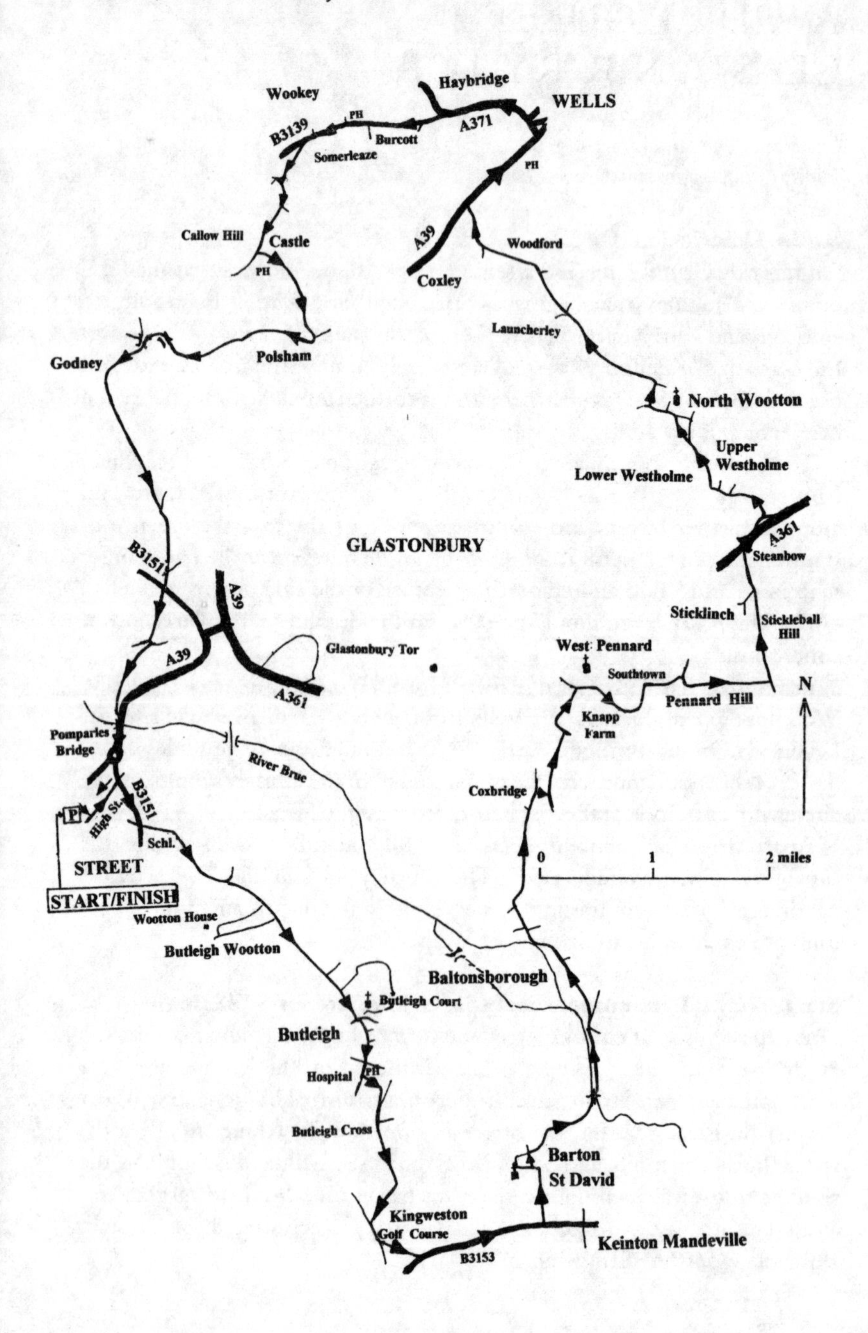

Points of interest

Street: The home of Clark's Shoe factory, which has a Shoe Museum and a modern factory outlet shopping mall.

Stage 1 Butleigh – Kingweston – Barton St David – Baltonsborough

The entrance to Butleigh is marked by an avenue of cedar trees extending to the left and right of the road. Beyond this to the left is Butleigh Court and cricket ground. Continue along the road which bypasses the centre of the village, across the crossroads with the Rose and Portcullis Inn on the left and turn left at the Butleigh hospital along Kingweston Road. Keep on this road as it winds its way up past Butleigh Cross on the right to a T-junction with the Kingweston to Street road. Turn left, passing the golf course on the left and take the first turn on the left. At the junction with the B3153 turn left and in Kenton Mandeville take the first turning on the left to Barton St David (1 mile). The road turns sharp left and then right before entering the village. The church is of particular interest. At the crossroads just beyond the sports ground turn right to Baltonsborough (2.5 miles). Keep on this road across a humpback bridge over the River Brue and continue alongside the river. Glastonbury Tor can be seen away to the left. Follow the road to Baltonsborough and at the crossroads in the centre of the village keep straight on.

Points of interest

Butleigh: first recorded in 821 when a West Saxon king made a gift of land at 'Buddekaulegh' to one of his followers. Butleigh Court was once the manor of the Grenville family. Robert Grenville built the Grenville Steam Engine in 1875, and which is now housed in the Industrial Museum in Bristol.

Keinton Mandeville: known for its quarrying of the blue lias stone which is seen in many buildings in Somerset, and for the birthplace of the Victorian actor Sir Henry Irving.

Barton St. David: birthplace of the forefathers of John Adams (1735-1826) who succeeded George Washington as President of the United States.

Baltonsborough: birthplace of St Dunstan in 909, Abbot of Glastonbury and later Archbishop of Canterbury.

Stage 2 Baltonsborough – Southtown – Steanbow – North Wootton – Wells

Leave Baltonsborough and continue to the first turn on the right at Coxbridge to West Pennard. This is a short road to a T-junction. Turn left to West Pennard (1.25 miles). The road twists and turns towards West Pennard which is identified by the tall church tower surmounted by a small spire. On the outskirts of the village turn right at the signpost to Southtown. The road climbs up Pennard Hill, through the farmyard of Knapp Farm, round a sharp left-hand bend and up a steep and narrow road between high grassed banks. Follow the road up to a sharp right-hand turn near a gate and ride along this flat road to a T-junction. Turn right and continue to another T-junction. Turn left and descend the steep Stickleball Hill past Stocklinch to Steanbow and the A361. Turn right and then take the first turn on the left to North Wootton (1.5 miles) and Wells (5.0 miles). The road runs parallel to the A361, passes across a river bridge and then turns left away from the A361. Pass through Lower Westholme (signposted) and keep straight on at the signpost indicating North Wootton. Follow the road round and at the T-junction turn left to Launcherley (1.5 miles) and Wells (3.75 miles). The church of North Wootton is seen over to the right. Keep on this road and follow it round a sharp-right hand bend. The road runs towards the high hill and at the next T-junction turn left to Wells. At the crossroads at Launcherley keep straight on to Woodford from where there are panoramic views over to Wells and the Mendips. Descend from here and at the A39 turn right to Wells.

Points of interest

North Wootton: a quiet farming village with a flourishing vineyard.

Wells: the 12th century Cathedral built on the site of an old Saxon Minster, together with the moated Bishop's Palace, the 14th century Vicars Close and the Market Place form the historic centre of the city. The Museum and Information Centre are important sources of information on the whole area of this tour.

Stage 3 Wells – Burcott – Polsham – Godney – Glastonbury – Street

Pass through the traffic lights in Wells, past the Sherston Inn on the right and at the mini-roundabout turn left down Princes Road. Pass through the traffic lights and take the A371 to Cheddar at the mini-roundabout. Keep straight on along Portway, past the Blue School on the right and at the roundabout keep to the left. At the division of the road take the left-hand road (B3139) to Burnham on Sea. Pass the Burcott Inn on the right and the gates of Somerleaze House on the left, and take the next turning on the left.

This signposted road to Fenny Castle and Godney runs at an angle to the B3139 and passes a school on the right. Continue to the junction, at a triangular grassed area, and turn left. There is no signpost at this junction. Pass down the narrow lane which bears round to the right below Callow Hill.

Keep on this road until it arrives at Castle and the Fenny Castle House and Country Inn. Turn left just before the Inn and continue to the T-junction in Polsham. Turn right to Godney (1.75 miles), passing Yew Tree Farm on the left and Folly Farm on the right. The road winds its way to

Godney passing Garslade Farm and crossing a bridge over a rhyne to a crossroads. Turn left to Glastonbury (3.0 miles) over another rhyne before passing through Godney. The road to Glastonbury follows a straight line for over a mile.

Keep straight on at the crossroads with the B3151 to another road junction. Ride directly across to join a road which passes through a derelict factory site before arriving at the junction with the A39. Turn right, across the Pomparles Bridge over the River Brue, and at the roundabout bear left into Street and back to the car park.

Points of interest

Godney: Site of an Iron Age Lake village. Details of the archeological finds are to be seen in the museum in Glastonbury.

Glastonbury: a place of pilgrimage wrapped in history, mystery and legend. The site of the earliest foundations of English Christianity. The Tor towers above the town and acts as a landmark for miles around. Places to visit include the Abbey, the Tribunal, Tor Hill, the Abbey Barn Rural Life Museum and the George and Pilgrim, an old pilgrim hostelry.

Wedmore to Brent Knoll Hill Fort

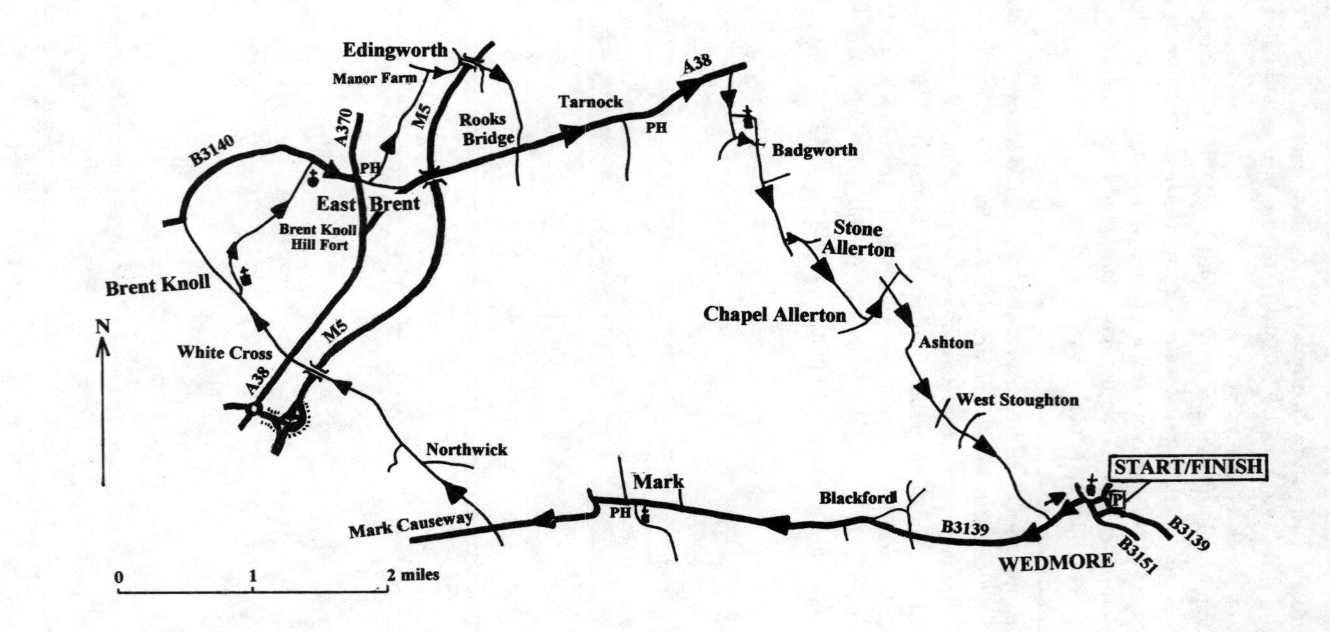

RIDE 11

WEDMORE TO BRENT KNOLL HILL FORT

Distance: 21 miles.
Journey time: approximately 4 hours easy riding.

Route Description
To appreciate this ride cyclists must go back in time and imagine that they are members of a Saxon community residing on the 'islet' of Wedmore, and that a journey is to be made across the Levels to the larger 'islet' of Brent Knoll, the return being made by a different route.

The journey begins in Wedmore and leaves the outpost of the 'islet' at Mark before travelling across the exposed Levels to the foot of the 'islet' of Brent Knoll. A climb to the summit of the Saxon hill fort is rewarded by a breathtaking panoramic view along the coast from Brean Down to the north to Selworthy Beacon above Minehead to the south. Inland there are the majestic Mendips, with the Cheddar Gorge clearly visible, whilst to the east the Levels, the many 'islets' including Avalon and the Tor are clearly seen. The return is made across the Levels to the higher ground at Badgeworth, and from there to Wedmore.

The journey is easy and essentially flat except for the ride over the Knoll. A climb to the summit on foot is well rewarded. The ride is one which offers constant change in scenery and with each change there comes a greater appreciation of this intriguing part of Somerset.

Start: (O.S. Landranger sheet 182, Grid reference ST435477)
Leave the exit of the car park in Wedmore and turn left to join the main street, called the Borough. Turn right and then first left up Church Street, passing the George Hotel and the church of St Mary on the right. Continue along the B3139 towards Burnham, passing the Wedmore Sports Ground on the right.
Points of interest
Wedmore: an island in ancient times and site of a peace treaty between King Alfred and the Dane, Guthrum, in 878. It is an attractive village formed around an open green. The church has a fine Jacobean pulpit, a mural of St Christopher and an impressive window commemorating the Jubilee of Queen Victoria.

Stage 1 Blackford – Mark – Brent Knoll
Brent Knoll is clearly visible as the road passes the village of Blackford and

down to a sharp left -hand bend. Continue along this road passing through Mark with the church and Pack Horse Inn on the left. On the outskirts of the village the road forms a sharp S-bend near the White Horse Inn. The road from this point is called Mark Causeway. Take the first turn on the right. The road passes through Northwick and on to a bridge over the M5 to a junction with the A38. Care has to be taken in crossing this busy road to join the road into the village of Brent Knoll.

Pass into the village and turn right down Church Lane and continue up to St Michael's church. The public footpath to the summit of the Knoll is situated a little way down the road from the church entrance.

Points of interest

Mark: an ancient farming village on the edge of the marshy Levels and at the end of the ridge from Wedmore. The Pack Horse Inn was formerly an important staging post for wool merchants travelling from the Mendips to the coast.

Brent Knoll: rises abruptly and dramatically from the Levels, a strategic observation point and hill fort in the Iron Age and a Saxon refuge from the Danish invaders. St Michael's church with its Norman doorway contains a number of medieval bench ends. They satirically depict the Abbot of Glastonbury as a wily fox, defrocked and later hanged, indicating the disrespect of the people for the covetous Abbot.

Stage 2 Brent Knoll – East Brent – Badgworth

On leaving the church ride downhill along the lane, bearing right along Hill Lane past the Woodlands Country Hotel. Continue up the steep hill. From the top the spire of East Brent church can be seen. The road runs beneath the summit of the Knoll where the defence ditches remain clearly defined. The views from this height are excellent but do not match those from the summit. At the junction with the B3140 in East Knoll turn right and pass through the village to the A370. Cross to join the road to Edingworth. Pass the Knoll Inn and turn immediately left by the the side of the inn. This road winds its way to a T-junction in Edingworth with Manor Farm on the left. Turn right and follow the road round the left hand bend and cross the bridge over the M5. The road forks at a short distance over the bridge. Take the road to the left and continue to the A38 at Rooks Bridge. Turn left onto the busy A38, pass the New Moon Inn on the right-hand side and take the next turning on the right to Chapel Allerton, 2.5 miles away. Brent Knoll can be seen to the right as the road forms an S-bend into the hamlet of Badgworth, whose church stands away to the left of the road.

Points of interest

East Brent: the church contains medieval glass, bench ends and a medieval wooden lectern.

Stage 3 Badgworth – Stoney Allerton – Chapel Allerton – Ashton – Wedmore

Continue along this flat road which begins to rise slightly as it approaches Stone Allerton (which has no sign). At the junction in the village turn left and follow the road as it rises slightly to a right-hand bend. Just round the bend there is a choice of roads. Do not follow the obvious road to the left but keep straight on, passing New House Farm on the right. This is the shortest way to Chapel Allerton. Keep straight on through this farmland area, which is raised slightly above the Levels. At the next T-junction turn left towards Weare. Pass through Chapel Allerton and at the next junction turn right towards Stoughton and Blackford. Pass through Ashton and continue on to a crossroads in West Stoughton. Ignore the signpost directions to Blackford and Highbridge and go diagonally across the road to join an unsignposted road. Keep straight on at the next crossroads to the T-junction with the B3139 opposite Tuckers West End Garage in Wedmore. Turn left here and follow the road down into the centre of Wedmore to the car park.

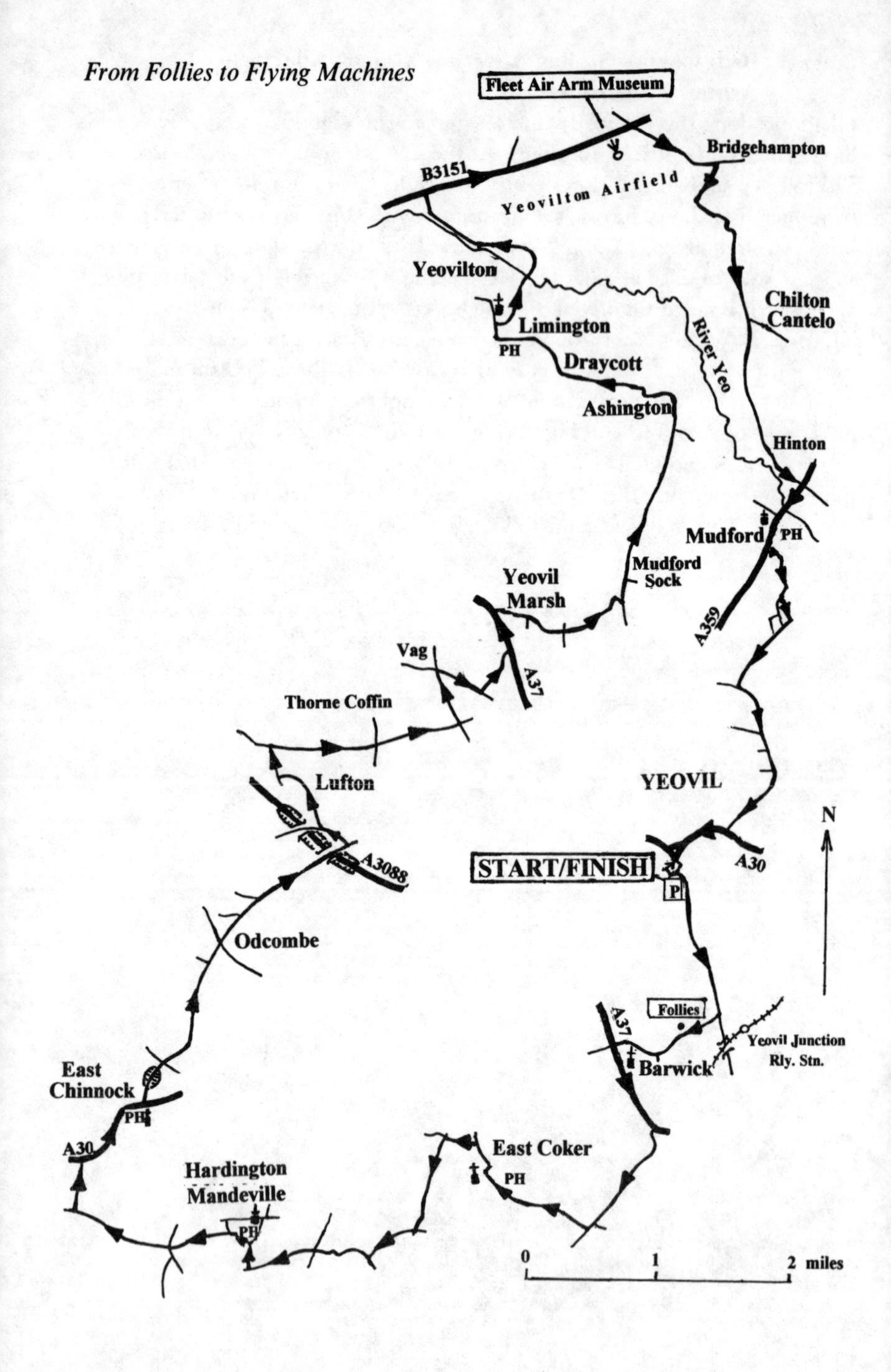
From Follies to Flying Machines
Fleet Air Arm Museum
Bridgehampton
B3151
Yeovilton Airfield
Yeovilton
Chilton
Cantelo
Limington
PH
Draycott
River Yeo
Ashington
Hinton
Mudford
PH
Mudford
Sock
Yeovil
Marsh
A359
Vag
A37
Thorne Coffin
Lufton
YEOVIL
N
A3088
START/FINISH
P
A30
Odcombe
Follies
A37
Yeovil Junction
Rly. Stn.
Barwick
East
Chinnock
PH
A30
East Coker
PH
Hardington
Mandeville
PH
0
1
2 miles

RIDE 12

FROM FOLLIES TO FLYING MACHINES

Distance: 34 miles.
Journey time: approximately 6 hours.

Route Description

From Yeovil the ride wends its way along by-roads to Barwick to view the 'Follies of Barwick' before moving on to the charming village of East Coker and its ties with the poet T. S. Eliot. Between East Coker and Hardington Mandeville the scenic beauty of Somerset and the border area of Dorset is seen at its best and is a fitting link between these handsome Hamstone villages.

The journey continues through West Chinnock and Odcombe before dropping down to Yeovil Marsh, Ashington, Limington and Yeovilton. It is necessary to use the B3151 to reach Bridgehampton, but in doing so there is an opportunity to visit the Fleet Air Arm Museum. The flat lanes from Bridgehampton through Chilton Cantelo to Mudford make for comfortable riding and relative freedom from traffic. The valley is surrounded by hills and it is the climb up from Mudford which brings the ride back to Yeovil.

Start: (O.S. Landranger sheets 183 and 194, Grid reference for sheet 183 ST561157)

Leave the car park, off Old Station Road in Yeovil, and turn left opposite the Alexandra Inn into Old Station Road. Follow the one-way system round to the right into Middle Street, and bear right at the sign to Barwick and Yeovil Junction Railway Station. Pass across the old railway bridge and continue along Newton Road to the turning just before the 30mph speed limit sign near the railway station. Turn right up this narrow unsignposted road between high rocky banks, until Jack the Treacle Eater, the first of the follies, is seen in the field to the right. The road passes the entrance to Barwick House, and two other follies, called Messiter's Cone and the Fish Tower, can be seen in the fields to the right. Barwick church is directly ahead. The road passes Little Barwick House and down a hill to a junction. Bear right along Church Lane past the church on the left and follow the road to the A37, the old Roman Road from Yeovil to Dorchester.

Points of interest

Yeovil: little left of earlier buildings, although the 14th century church of

St Johns still survives. An important agricultural centre since medieval times and the glove making industry begun in the 14th century still flourishes. In more recent times the introduction of engineering by the Petter family developed into Westland Helicopters.

Stage 1 Barwick – East Coker – Hardington Mandeville

Turn left onto the A37 and continue along the road to the fourth folly called the Needle or Pinnacle which stands near the edge of the road. Turn right here towards East Coker (1.75 miles). Ignore the turn to the left and a little further on take the first turn to the right leading to East Coker (0.75 miles). Keep straight on through the village past the Helyar Arms on the right to where the road bears to the right. It is worthwhile stopping here to visit the almshouses and the church on the left before continuing the journey. Return to the main road through the village and ride round a sharp left-hand bend and take the first turn on the left (unsignposted). The road passes a series of industrial buildings on the right and the village hall, before heading out into the country to a signpost. Turn left towards Pendomer and follow the road as it rises and runs alongside the Coker Court land on the left. From the top of the hill the road runs downhill providing wonderful views of the wooded Dorset countryside to the left. Bear to the right at the next minor junction following the direction to Pendomer (1.0 mile). The road runs along a ridge separating two valleys. At the next signpost keep straight on to Hardington Mandeville (1.25 miles). Keep straight on at the next crossroads and take the next turn on the right into the village of Hardington Mandeville and follow the road to a T-junction. (Refreshments can be obtained from the Mandeville Arms which is directly ahead near the church of St Mary).

Points of interest

Barwick: best known for the four follies in the park of Barwick House: the Needle, Messiter's Cone, the Fish Tower and Jack the Treacle Eater (a lock-up on top of a roughly shaped arch and topped by a lead figure depicting Hermes, the messenger of the Gods).

East Coker: one of the most delightful villages in Somerset with mellow Hamstone cottages. Coker Court (13th century) and the 17th century Helyar Almshouses stand close to the parish church of St Michael, first documented in 1276. The church contains the ashes of and a plaque to the poet T. S. Eliot whose ancestor Andrew Eliot emigrated to America in 1660, settled in Salem and was a juror at the famous Witch Trials.

Stage 2 Hardington Mandeville – East Chinnock – Odcombe – Lufton – Yeovil Marsh

Turn left at the T-junction and follow the road towards Haselbury Plucknett. Ignore the turn on the right which leads down into the valley and at the next crossroads keep straight on. Take the next turning on the right marked by a small grassed triangle of land. The road runs downhill and East Chinnock can be seen ahead. Pass Cott Farm on the right and turn right at the A30. Follow the road along the outskirts of East Chinnock, past the Portman Arms on the right, and turn left to Odcombe (1.5 miles) opposite the church on the right.

The road climbs up between high rocky banks and at the crossroads at the top, keep straight on to Odcombe. At the next crossroads cross directly to continue along the road which runs along the outskirts of Odcombe. Pass the entrance to Brympton House and cross the bridge over the A3088.

At the next Give Way sign turn left towards Montecute and take the first turn on the right to Lufton (1.0 mile). Pass Lufton Manor on the right and bear left to a T-junction. Turn right, and right again at the next T-junction (no signpost) and follow the road to a crossroads. Keep straight on and to next crossroads on the outskirts of Yeovil. Turn left towards Vagg and turn right towards Yeovil at the next crossroads near Vagg Farm. Take the next turn on the left to Yeovil Marsh. At the junction with the A37 (Ilchester to Yeovil road) turn left and ride down to the first turning on the right to Yeovil Marsh.

Points of interest

Brympton d'Evercy: a beautiful Elizabethan Manor house built of yellow Hamstone containing the longest staircase in England. The nearby 15th century Priest House is now a museum and cider mill; a sheltered vineyard produces and sells wine.

Stage 3 Yeovil Marsh – Limington – Yeovilton – Chilton Cantelo – Mudford – Yeovil

Pass through the village of Yeovil Marsh towards Mudford Sock. Ignore the right turn to Mudford Sock and keep straight on to Ashington, Draycott and Limington, passing the Lamb and Lark Inn on the left. Just before the church in Limington turn right to Yeovilton (0.75 miles) and follow the road as it winds its way to the village. The road makes a sweeping left-hand bend from the bridge over the River Yeo before straightening to run alongside the river on the left, and the end of the airfield of the Royal Naval Air Station on the right. At the B3151 turn right passing H.M.S. *Heron*, the Royal Naval Air Station and Fleet Air Arm Museum.

Turn right at the next crossroads to Bridgehampton (0.5 miles). After the bridge just beyond the village take the first turn on the right to Chilton Cantelo (1.0 mile) passing near the other end of the airfield. This area is the valley of the River Yeo. The road follows an exaggerated zig-zag path prior to crossing the Hornsey Brook. At the division of the road in Chilton Cantelo bear right and continue to Hinton and the junction with the A359.

Turn right, pass over the River Yeo and climb up through Mudford. Turn left just before the speed-limit sign near the top of the village. Follow this road through a housing estate to open country, bear right round a sharp bend and take the first turn on the left by the postbox. At the next junction turn right and climb the hill to Primrose Lane and the junction with Lyde Road. Turn left and ride down to the mini-roundabout on the A30 Sherborne to Yeovil Road. Bear right and follow the road to Middle Street. Turn left along Newton Road and return to the car park via the one-way system.

Points of interest

Yeovilton: the Fleet Air Arm Museum houses a superb collection of aircraft telling the story of naval aviation, including the Gulf war, and a Concorde prototype.

RIDE 13

THROUGH THE FARMLAND OF SOUTH SOMERSET

Distance: 37 miles.
Journey time: approximately 6-7 hours.

Route Description

The maze of minor roads and narrow lanes in this rolling farmland is ideal for exploration by bicycle. The lovely villages and hamlets with their abundance of thatched hamstone houses are a source of constant pleasure. This is just one of the many routes possible, and as the ride progresses from Chard through the small villages of Cudworth, Higher Chillington and Dinnington the beauty of the whole area can be truly appreciated. A return from the remote hamlets to the more familiar ones occurs at Norton-sub-Hamdon and Stoke-sub-Hamdon, whilst from Montacute there is a visit to the source of this glorious hamstone on Ham Hill.

Chiselborough, West Chinnock and Merriott are the last sizeable villages before the ride returns to the narrow lanes and brief use is made of the A30 to climb to the top of St. Rayn Hill and the lanes leading to Purtington. The Cricket St Thomas Wildlife Park can be seen from the minor road that leads from Purtington to Winsham, a small village near the Somerset/Dorset border.

From Winsham the journey to Chard passes through Ammerham to the River Exe and the entrance to Forde Abbey for those who may wish to make a visit. The route never leaves Somerset but merely brushes against the county boundary before the final stage of the journey to Chard. This is a ride for cyclists of diverse interests and varying cycling abilities.

Start: (O.S.Landranger sheet 193, Grid refence 322084)

Turn right at the exit to the car park in Boden Street, Chard, and at the main street (Fore Street) turn right. At the mini-roundabout near Chard School turn left along Furnham Road (the A358 to Ilminster and Taunton), and just beyond the Ship Inn turn right along Chaffcombe Road. Ignore the turn on the right and keep straight on with the reservoir to the right. The road bears right round the head of the reservoir, past the Somerset County Council Recycling Centre and on to a road junction. Turn left and keep straight on at the next turning on the right (to Chaffcombe). The road runs downhill and bears sharp left by Chaffcombe Farm Gate and climbs up Sprays Hill. At the top there are wonderful views over the surrounding landscape. Keep straight on where a road comes in from the

Through the Farmland of South Somerset

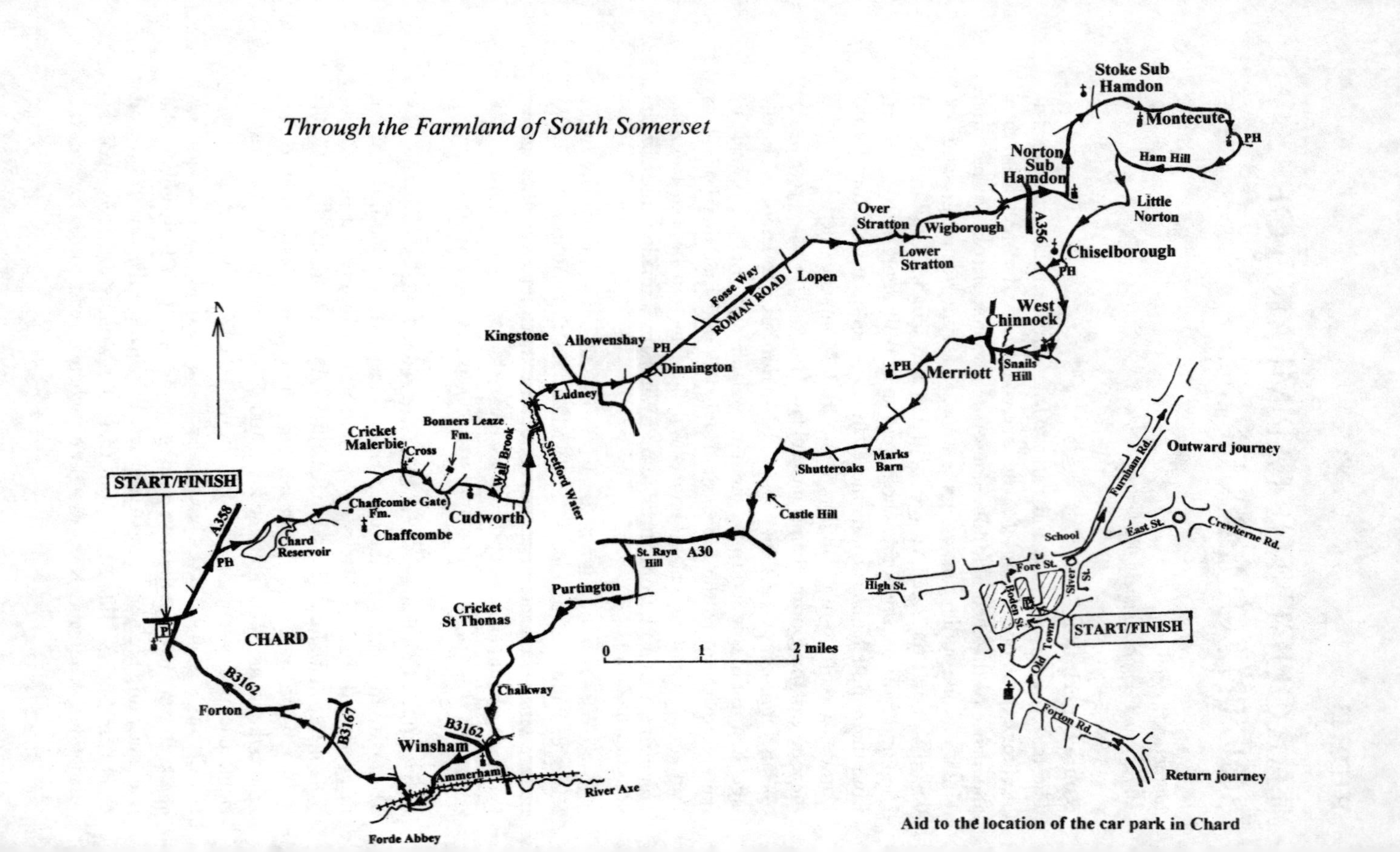

Aid to the location of the car park in Chard

left, and to the next crossroads which is marked by a stone cross (Cricket Cross) standing in the corner of the field opposite.

Points of interest

Chard: the High Street dominates the centre of town with the Manor Court House, the Choughs Hotel, the Guildhall and the old School being attractive reminders of Chard's past. The Museum is a source of information on the industrial history of the town and of John Stringfellow, the avaition pioneer.

Stage 1 Cricket Cross – Cudworth – Ludney – Dinnington – Lopen

Pass straight over the crossroads and ride towards Cudworth (1 mile). Disregard the next road on the left and keep straight on along this picturesque section past the entrance to Bonners Leaze Farm. At the next junction bear left downhill and take the first turn on the right into Cudworth and ride towards the small church of St Michael. Carry on from the church past the farmhouse on the left and down the narrow lane to a bridge over the Wall Brook. At the T-junction turn left (unsignposted) towards Ludney. On the ridge ahead there is a screen of poplar trees standing to the rear of a large orchard. Ride across a steel bridge over Stretford Water and at the T-junction turn left to Ludney (0.75 miles). Follow the road as it passes across a second steel bridge and at the next junction bear right to Ludney and Allowenshay. Follow the road, ignoring the turn to the right at the grassy triangle, to the junction with the road to Crewkerne. Turn right and take the first turn on the left to Dinnington. This is a narrow lane running between high tree-lined banks. Ignore the road coming from the left and at the next junction bear left to Lopen (2.25 miles). Disregard the turnings to the right and keep straight on into Dinnington passing the Rose and Crown Inn. Travel along the Fosse Way, the Roman road, to Lopen.

Points of interest

Cudworth: a village near the Fosse Way, an old Roman road. It is mainly agricultural but in former times was involved in cloth-making and glove-making.

Lopen: situated on the Fosse Way, the local industry being mainly agriculture and cloth-making. Associated with Cardinal Wolsey, who as tutor to the Earl of Dorset's sons was placed in the village stocks for being too disorderly at the Lopen Fair.

Stage 2 Lopen – Over Stratton – Lower Stratton – Wigborough – Norton-sub-Hamdon

Continue for 1.5 miles to a crossroads in Lopen and cross over diagonally to Broomfield Lane. Please note that great care has to be used in crossing this road due to the sharp S-bend in the road.

Broomfield Lane is narrow and runs between high tree-lined banks to Over Stratton. Turn left at the main road running through Over Stratton, and turn right almost immediately to Lower Stratton and Wigborough. This turning is near the corner where the main road bears left. Follow the road to Lower Stratton and at the next junction bear right and carry on into Wigborough. At the signpost, in Wigborough, turn left to Norton-sub-Hamdon. Follow this flat road as it bears to the right and at the A356 cross directly onto the road into Norton-sub-Hamdon. The village lies beneath the high ridge of Ham Hill. Take the first turn on the left (New Road) to Stoke-sub-Hamdon.

Points of interest

Norton-sub-Hamdon: the church of St Mary the Virgin built by Henry VII in the 15th century. The Pigeon House in the churchyard can house 400 nests and is unique.

Stage 3 Stoke-sub-Hamdon – Montacute – Little Norton – Chesilborough

Turn right at the junction with the main road through Stoke-sub-Hamdon past the Priory (NT) and the centre of the village on the way to Montacute. There are superb views to the left of the road to Montacute. Pass the main gates to Montacute House on the left and bear sharp left at the church. Follow the road to the village centre and the visitors' entrance to Montacute House. Pass the Phelips Arms and take the first turn on the right, called Townsend. The road winds its way up between tree-lined banks to a T-junction at the top. Turn right to enter the Ham Hill Country Park and pass the Lime Kiln Car Park with its lovely views over the landscape. Just before the second viewing point the minor road to Little Norton turns sharp left and descends quite steeply to the village.

Pass through the village and turn left to Chesilborough at the next junction. Enter the village past Manor Farm on the right and turn right at the next junction in the village. Pass the church on the right and the Cat's Head Inn on the left and continue to the crossroads on the edge of the village. Turn left to West Chinnock.

Points of interest

Stoke-sub-Hamdon: 17th century houses with mullioned windows. The church of St Mary, East Stoke, dates from the 11th century. Stoke House Priory (NT) in North Street, built in the 14th and 15th centuries.

Montacute House (NT): built by the Phelips family, and an excellent example of Elizabethan architecture.

Stage 4 Chesilborough – West Chinnock – Merriott – Purtington

At the next road junction bear right down through West Chinnock. Cross over Chinnock Brook, pass the Muddled Man Inn, on past the church on the right to the signpost to Merriott (2.0 miles). Turn right up Duck Pool Lane and at the junction bear left to Snails Hill. At the T-junction with the A356 turn right and then first left to Merriott (1 mile), passing the John Scott Nurseries on the left. Disregard the turn to the right and carry straight on through the village to a crossroads. Go directly across onto Moorlands Road and keep straight on and up past the entrance to Marks Barn to a crossroads at Shutteroaks. Go directly across along this lane and at the T-junction turn left towards Castle Hill, a grass and bracken covered hill. The road drops down, crosses a stream before climbing and following the contours of the hill in a left-handed curve, and through woods to the A30. There are superb views along this part of the ride.

Turn right up St Rayn Hill to the second turning on the left, signposted to Purtington. Turn left and at the next crossroads turn right to Purtington. This is a very narrow and little used lane lined with high banks. Just before entering the hamlet of Purtington turn left along a road which rises steeply in a curving right-hand bend and bypasses the hamlet.

Points of interest

Chesilborough: a village surrounded by five hills. The church of St. Peter is one of the few churches in Somerset with a spire.

Merriott: lies in a fertile area and in the past flax was grown for the cloth industry; gardening and 'nurseries' are recorded as far back as 1375. John Scott's Nursery maintains this tradition.

Stage 5 Purtington – Winsham – Forton – Chard

Carry straight on along the edge of a wood on the right and where the tree line ends the Cricket St. Thomas Wildlife Park can be seen to the right. The road turns sharp left and drops down to a sharp right-hand bend before continuing downhill to cross over a stream. The road then climbs past a house on the left at Chalkway to a right-hand bend before dropping down to a junction in Winsham. Ignore the road to the right and go straight ahead to a second junction. Turn right along Fore Street, passing the United Reform Church on the right, to a crossroads. Cross the B3162 to the road (Western Way) on the left of the War Memorial. From here Forde Abbey is 1.75 miles and Chard Junction is 3.0 miles. Continue along this road and at the junction of the roads in Ammerham bear left across a railway bridge towards the River Axe, which forms the Somerset/Dorset border. At the next T-junction, just in Somerset, turn right and cross the railway bridge once more. (To visit Forde Abbey turn left at this junction to the entrance, a short distance down the road.)

Continue on and take the first turn on the left at a triangle of grass. This road rises past Leigh House, a large house on the right. Cross the B3167 and keep straight on, passing the Alpine Grove camping site on the right. At the junction with the B3162 turn left. Cross an old railway bridge and follow the road round a sharp right-hand bend into Forton, passing Forton Lodge on the right. Leave the village and continue along Forton Road to the junction in Chard. Turn right at the church and ride down Old Town. At the junction with Silver Street turn left and then right into Boden Street (see inset map).

Points of interest

Cricket St Thomas: the present manor house designed in the 1780's after the original house was destroyed by fire, was built for Admiral Hood. The wildlife park extends for a 1000 acres and includes a wide range of animals and birds.

Winsham: 13th century church with a picture of the Crucifixion painted on wood. The village was once important in the cloth industry and the village cross was a meeting place for traders.

Forde Abbey: near Ammerham and just in Dorset. An 800 year old Cistercian abbey, little altered; became a private residence in the 17th century. Houses the famous Mortlake Tapestries. Thirty acres of gardens open all year. House open March to October.

RIDE 14

A RIDE TO CAMELOT

Distance: 34 miles.
Journey time: approximately 6 hours easy riding.

Route Description

The ride begins in the historic Roman town of Ilchester and follows the flat farmland roads to the village of Mudford. The landscape then changes to gently rounded hills, a geographical feature which continues to South Cadbury and beyond to the village of Woolston. Thereafter it returns to a relatively flat landscape. There is a steep hill leading from the village of Sandford Orcas to Corton Denham and another leading from Lower Woolston to the village of Woolston.

The route provides continuing interest, the opportunity to visit Cadbury Castle – the Camelot of Arthurian legend – panoramic views, delightful villages and a true appreciation of why Cadbury Castle held such a strategic position in the surrounding landscape in pre-Roman Britain.

Start: (O.S. Landranger sheet 183, Grid reference ST522224)

From the car park in Ilchester, turn right and head east out of the town past the cemetery, towards Limington. After about 1.5 miles the road bears sharp right, passing Limington church on the left. Carry straight on, ignoring the road to Yeovilton. The road then bears sharp left past the Lamb and Lark Inn and Draycott Farm into Ashington, passing the church and Ashington Manor Farm. After leaving Ashington take the signposted road to Mudford.

Points of interest

Limington: the church of St Mary is remembered for its association with Cardinal Wolsey, who as Thomas Wolsey was presented in 1500 to the living of Limington which he held until 1509, although he resided in the village for only a year before being appointed Chaplain to the Archbishop of Canterbury in 1501.

Stage 1 Mudford – Trent – Sandford Orcas

At the junction of the Mudford road and the A359 turn left towards Marston Magna. At the next crossroads turn right to Trent and after about 0.75 miles turn right again. Cross over the railway bridge and take the second turning on the left to Trent at a grassed triangle of land. The Rose and Crown Inn is on the right and the church of St Andrew on the left. Continue to the signposted (Sherborne) junction near the Almshouses and

A Ride to Camelot

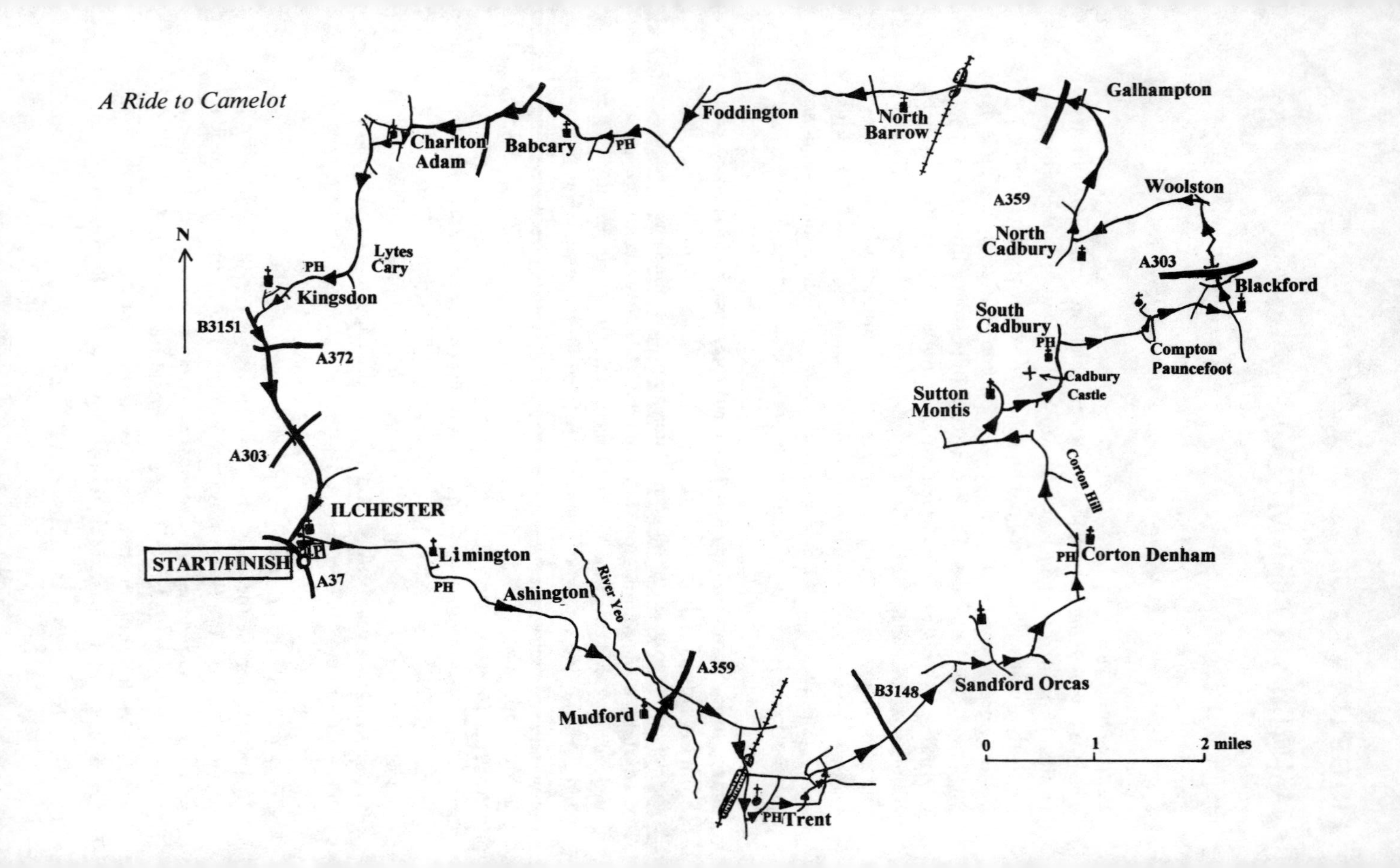

turn right. Take the fourth turning on the left at Rigg Lane, opposite a red telephone box. Bear round to the right and take the second turning on the left which leads to a crossroads. Turn right and continue to the B3148. Cross the B3148 to the road to Sandford Orcas 1.25 miles away. After approximately 0.75 miles the road descends to a sharp left turn. Pass Glenholme Nurseries and turn right at the next junction. This road dips down between high, tree-lined banks to a T-junction in the village. Turn right and at the end of the village take the left hand fork to Corton Denham.

Points of interest

Trent: St Andrew's church was possibly begun in the 13th century. Lord Fisher of Lambeth, the former Archbishop of Canterbury who conducted the Coronation service of Queen Elizabeth II, lived in Trent Rectory on his retirement and regularly conducted services in the church. His robes can be seen in the south transept together with a slate tablet recording his life. The Chantry at the entrance to the churchyard was where the chantry priest lived.

Stage 2 Sandford Orcas – Corton Denham – Sutton Montis – South Cadbury

The road to Corton Denham from Sandford Orcas is unsignposted and steep, rising steadily to a junction. Turn left and keep straight on into Corton Denham below Corton Hill. Pass the Queen's Arms Inn on the left and the Church of St Andrew further down on the right. On leaving the village follow the main road which rises and bears left, still running beneath Corton Hill. At the next junction there is a signpost to Whitcombe farm. From this point there is an impressive view of the plateau of the Cadbury Hill Fort, with the prominent defensive ditches on its slopes. Continue on, down to another junction. Ignore the right-hand turn and follow the sign to Little Weston. At the next junction turn right into Sutton Montis. Ride through the village and turn right at the sign to South Cadbury. This section of the journey runs close beneath Cadbury Hill Fort and into the South Cadbury. The road passes the church of Thomas a' Becket, and at the Red Lion Inn turn right to Compton Pauncefoot (1 mile).

Points of interest

Sutton Montis: Abbey House (near church), Parsonage Farm (17th century).

South Cadbury: a tour of Cadbury Hill Fort can be made via Castle Lane (south of the church).

Stage 3 South Cadbury – Compton Pauncefoot – Blackford – Woolston – North Cadbury

Pass through the village of Compton Pauncefoot noting the unusual crescent of three-storied buildings on the left. At the T-junction, the church can be seen down to the left. Turn right here for Blackford and continue up the tree-lined hill with a valley on the left. At the next junction (unsignposted) take the road almost directly opposite and complete the short remaining distance to Blackford. Turn left at the main road through the village, and follow the sign to Wincanton up a hill to a crossroads. Cross the road and pass under the A303. Ride down to Lower Woolston, and then climb up to the village of Woolston. At the top turn left into the village and at the signposted junction Galhampton/North Cadbury follow the North Cadbury road.

This road is flat and enters North Cadbury on the Woolston Road passing St Michael's church and the Tudor manor house on the left. Turn right along Cary Road, past the Catash Inn on the right, and on through the village to a marked sharp bend bearing to the left. At this point take the signposted route to Galhampton.

Points of interest

Compton Pauncefoot, Blackford, Woolston and North Cadbury are all attractive villages well worth exploring.

Stage 4 North Cadbury – Galhampton – North Barrow – Babcary – Charlton Adam – Kingsdon – Ilchester

The road to Galhampton is quite delightful and passes a large house on the right with two attractive waterfalls in the garden. At the T-junction on the outskirts of the village turn left. Continue to the A359 and cross directly to join the road to North Barrow. There are superb panoramic views here of the Somerset landscape including Glastonbury Tor. This road runs steeply down to a right-hand bend, over a railway bridge, and on through the village of North Barrow to a crossroads. Disregard the signs to South Barrow and Lovington and take the road directly opposite which leads to Foddington. Along this road on the right, there is a large grey stone house with two large red brick chimneys. The road winds its way to a T-junction. Turn left to Babcary and continue to another T-junction. Turn right into the village, passing the Red Lion Inn on the left and continue on to the A37. Turn left and take the second turning on the right to Charlton Adam. Care should be taken here as the turning is at a sharp bend in the road.

Follow the road into the village passing the Fox and Hounds Inn on the left and bear sharp left at the next junction. Just past the village store on the left, leave the main road and take the narrow road that runs straight ahead towards a large house with a high wall directly ahead. Follow the road as it veers to the right, and at the next T-junction turn left passing a garage on the left. Take the Kingsdon road at the mini-roundabout. Continue to Lytes Cary and turn right to Kingsdon. On entering the village take the lower road past the yellow-painted Village Hall, following the road round the Kingsdon Inn which sweeps left and then right to B3151. Turn left and continue to the A372. Turn right and then immediately left over the A303 and into Ilchester.

Points of interest

Lytes Cary (NT): a typical Somerset stone-built manor house with its own 15th century chapel.

Kingsdon: a very attractive village.

Ilchester: once an important Roman town sited where the Fosse Way from Lincoln to Axmouth was joined by a road from the Bristol Channel to Dorchester. Ilchester was the birthplace of Roger Bacon in 1214, a Franciscan friar who displayed a scientific vision far in advance of his era. Further information can be obtained from the Museum in the High Street.

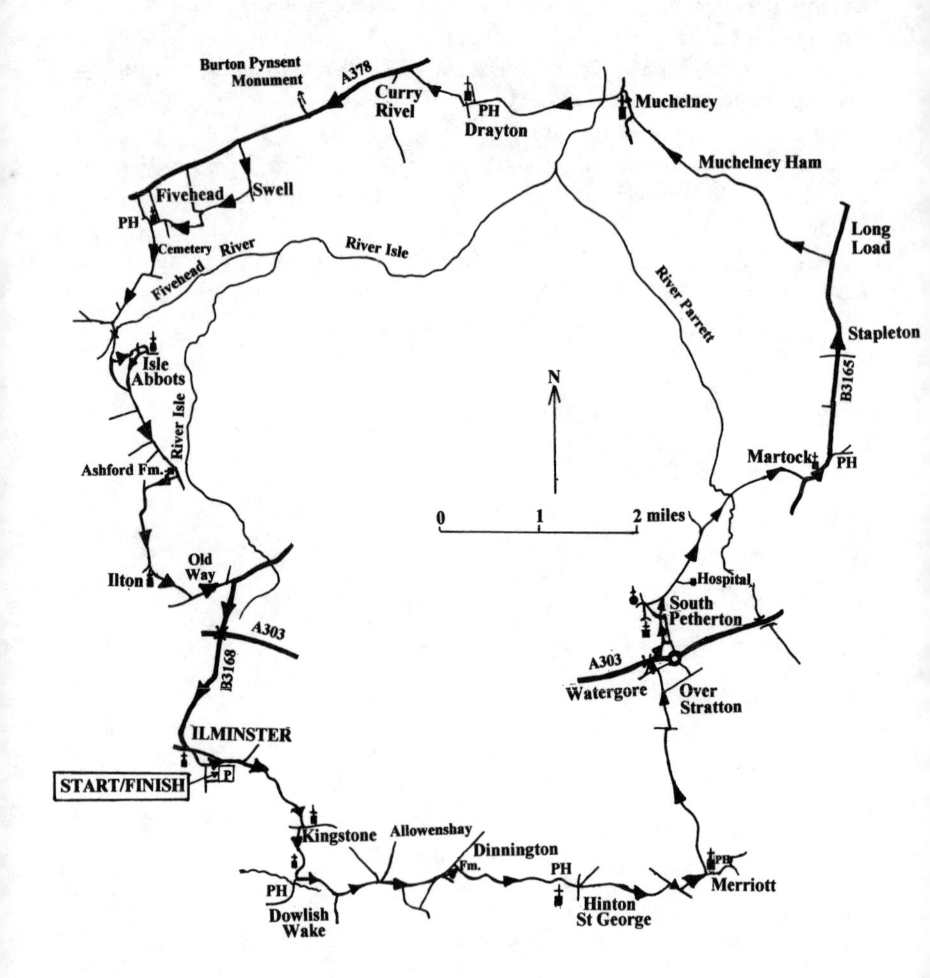
South Somerset Villages
Burton Pynsent Monument
A378
Curry Rivel
PH
Drayton
Muchelney
Muchelney Ham
Long Load
Fivehead
Swell
PH
Cemetery
River
Fivehead
River Isle
River Parrett
Stapleton
Isle Abbots
N
B3165
River Isle
Martock
PH
Ashford Fm.
0
1
2 miles
Old Way
Ilton
Hospital
South Petherton
A303
B3168
A303
Watergore
Over Stratton
ILMINSTER
START/FINISH
P
Kingstone
Allowenshay
Dinnington
Fm.
PH
PH
Merriott
PH
Dowlish Wake
Hinton St George

RIDE 15

SOUTH SOMERSET VILLAGES

Distance: 34 miles.
Journey time: approximately 6 hours.

Route Description

Ilminster, an interesting town with an attractive market place, is an excellent setting for the start of a tour that reveals the beauty and charm of this moorland area of South Somerset. It is characterised by the maze of intersecting lanes that link the villages. The area is fairly flat and provides an easy ride. The only steep hill is that leading up to the outskirts of Ilminster on the return journey. The remainder are small hills that pose no problems and provide numerous vantage points over this lovely part of Somerset.

Start: (O.S. Landranger sheet 193, Grid reference ST362143)

Leave the car park in Shudrick Lane, Ilminster, and turn right at the junction with Ditton Street. At the Give Way sign turn right up East Street, past the pillared market house to the junction at the top of the hill. Turn right in the direction of Seavington St Michael and after a short distance turn right to Kingstone.

Stage 1 Dowlish Wake – Dinnington – Hinton St George – Merriott

Follow the Kingstone road for about 1 mile to a crossroads. Turn right here and then almost immediatey left onto the Dowlish Wake road, which winds down past the church to a signpost in the village. (For a visit to the Perry Cider Mill pass over the ford near the signpost and take the first right turn to the mill). To continue the journey return to the signpost and follow the Chillington road to a T-junction.

Turn left towards Allowenshay. Continue until the junction with the road from Kingstone. Turn right towards Crewkerne. After about 300 yards the road bears sharp right, and at this point take the minor signposted road to Dinnington.This narrow road runs below high banks to a road junction. Turn left and follow the signposted direction to Hinton St George (1.25 miles). Soon there is a another signpost to Hinton St George. This road bears to the right at an angle and leads down a very narrow road to a junction opposite a farm. Turn right and continue to Hinton St George. This route offers panoramic views of the moors.

Ride through the village along West Street past the Poullett Arms, over the crossroads and on towards Merriott. At the next T-junction turn right and then first left along Church Street into Merriott. Refreshments can be obtained at the King's Head Inn, just beyond the church (approx. 0.25 miles).

Points of interest

Dowlish Wake: delightful old hamstone village with a ford and stream. The church of St Andrew contains the tomb of Captain John Speke, the explorer who discovered the source of the Nile. Perrys Cider Mills is open all year round for cider sampling.

Hinton St George: charming hamstone village, ancestral home of the Poullett family and the home of Henry Fowler whilst compiling the Oxford English Dictionary.

Merriott: (see Ride 13).

Stage 2 Merriott – Over Stratton – South Petherton – Martock

Turn left just before the church to Over Stratton. At the entrance to the village there are large orchards on both sides of the road. Pass through the village and follow the sign to South Petherton, passing the Royal Oak on the right. Continue to the T-junction and turn left towards Lopen. Take the first turn on the right in Watergore and cross over the A303 into South Petherton. Ride along the main street with the Brewer's Arms on the right, through the centre of the village to a signpost to Martock. Follow this road down Silver Street to a Give Way sign and bear left up the hill out of the village, passing the hospital on the right. Continue along this road and over the River Parrett to the B3165. Turn left and follow to Stapleton and from there to Long Load.

Points of interest

South Petherton: formerly an old Saxon town once the property of the West Saxon kings.

Stage 3 Martock – Muchelney – Drayton – Curry Rivel – Swell – Fivehead

Take the first turning on the left along Long Load and continue to Muchelney (2.25 miles) via Muchelney Ham. There is a clear view of the Burton Pynsent monument at Curry Rivel. Turn right when the road reaches a junction in Muchelney. The Abbey will be seen to the left. Follow the road round a sharp left-hand bend to the church of St.Peter and St. Paul. The Priest's House is opposite the church. Take the signposted road to Drayton. In the village pass the church of St Catherine on the right and the Drayton Arms opposite. Continue along this road into Curry Rivel to the A378. Turn left and continue through the village. Whilst in Curry Rivel it is worthwhile visiting the Burton Pynsent monument for the view over the Somerset Levels and of the manor, which has strong associations with William Pitt the Elder. Access to the monument is from the road to Staithe and

Heal indicated by a signpost on the left hand side of the A378 near the outskirts of Curry Rivel. Follow this road for 0.2 miles to a large wrought iron gate on the left. Open the gate and cross to the gate leading to the field on the left. A footpath leads up the side of the field to a stile and access to the monument.

Continue the journey on the A378, and after approximately 1.25 miles turn left down the steep signposted road to Swell. From there travel to Fivehead and follow the signs to Isle Abbots. Pass the church in Fivehead and turn left past the Village Hall. Carry straight on past 'The Manse', a house with an ornate gateway, and the cemetery. At the next junction turn right to Isle Abbots. Keep left at the next junction. Cross the Fivehead River and take the first turning on the left into Isle Abbots. Follow the road round to the church of St Mary the Virgin. The tower of this church is considered one of the finest in the county and this corner of the village is particularly beautiful. Return directly through the village to rejoin the road to Ilton.

Points of interest

Martock: beautiful hamstone buildings: All Saints Church famous for its magnificent roof, Treasurer's House (NT), Church House (formerly Old Court House and Grammar School founded 1661), Market House, Manor House.

Muchelney: means 'great island', lying between the Rivers Parrett and Yeo. Remains of the 7th century Abbey, fine church with painted wagon roof, 12th century Priest's House (NT).

Curry Rivel: associated with the Pitt family. Magnificent 15th century church, Burton Pynsent Monument, a 140 foot monument designed by Capability Brown at Sir William Pitt's request in memory of Sir William Burton Pynsent, who had left his estate to Pitt.

Fivehead: Saxon village with fine views over the Levels.

Stage 4 Isle Abbots – Ilton – Ilminster

Follow the road to Ilton and take the fourth turning on the right by Ashford Farm and take this road to Ilton. Pass through the village to a T-junction. Turn left along Old Way and at the B3168 turn right for Ilminster. Cross over the A303 passing the entrance to Dillington House prior to climbing the steep hill to the outskirts of Ilminster. There are superb views from the hill. The road drops down to the George Hotel in the centre of Ilminster.

Points of interest

Ilton: associated with Sir Nicholas Wadham who founded Wadham College, Oxford, and has fine examples of almshouses.

From Ilminster to the Blackdowns

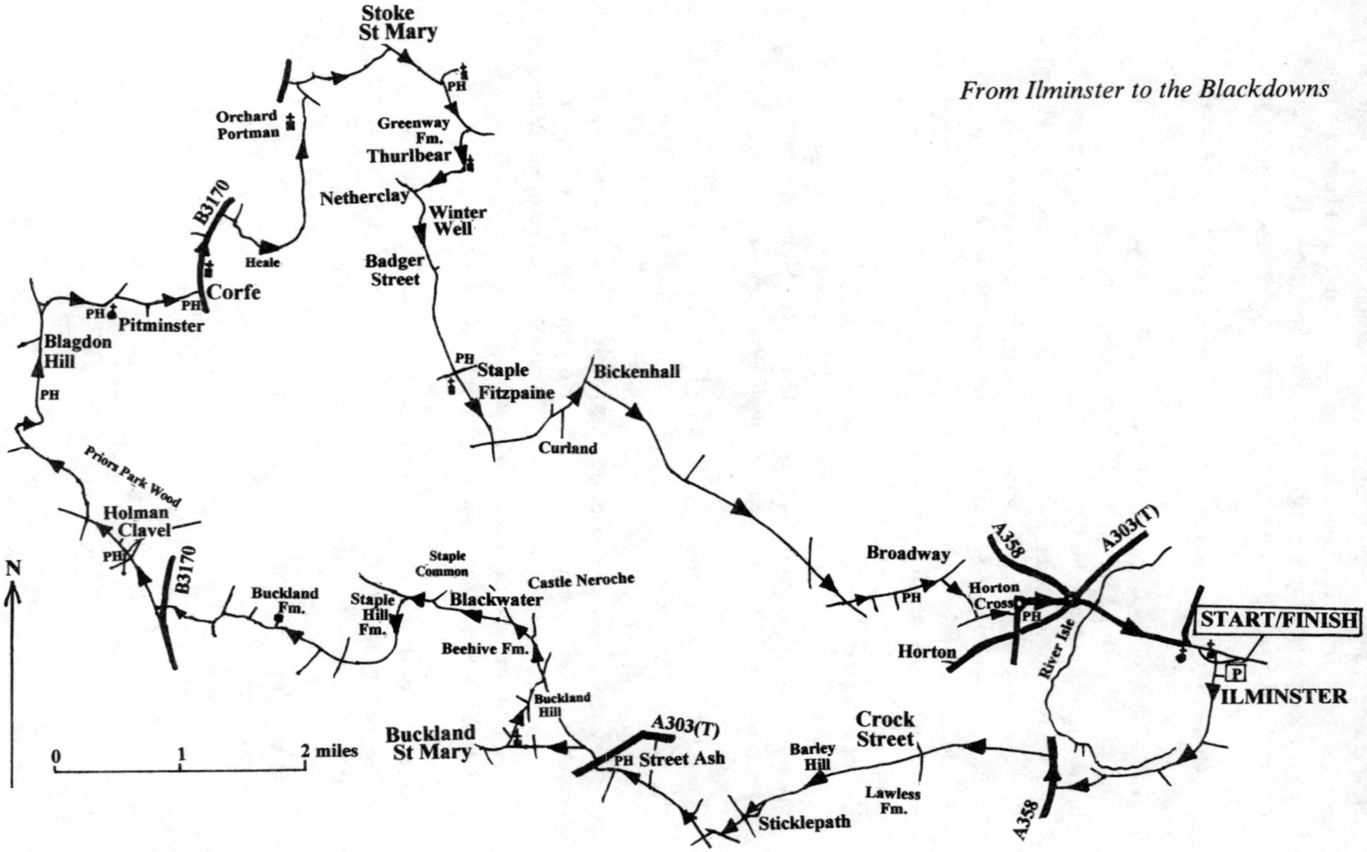

Stoke St Mary
PH
Orchard Portman
Greenway Fm.
Thurlbear
Netherclay
Winter Well
Badger Street
B3170
Heale
Corfe
PH
Pitminster
PH
Blagdon Hill
PH
Staple Fitzpaine
PH
Bickenhall
Curland
Priors Park Wood
Holman Clavel
PH
B3170
N
Buckland Fm.
Staple Common
Staple Hill Fm.
Blackwater
Castle Neroche
Beehive Fm.
Buckland Hill
Buckland St Mary
A303(T)
PH
Street Ash
0
1
2 miles
Broadway
PH
A358
A303(T)
Horton Cross
PH
Horton
River Isle
START/FINISH
P
ILMINSTER
Crock Street
Barley Hill
Lawless Fm.
Sticklepath
A358

RIDE 16

FROM ILMINSTER TO THE BLACKDOWNS

Distance: 33 miles.
Journey time: approximately 6-7 hours.

Route Description
The overall impression of this part of Somerset is of a sparsely populated area with deep valleys and densely wooded hillsides.The narrow lanes and continually changing terrain make this cycle ride one of continuing surprises. The tour starts from Ilminster and the climb up into the Blackdowns begins from Crock Street and reaches a peak near Sticklepath, before dropping gently down to Buckland St Mary. The route then moves to Blackwater where the rider is again in the undulating Blackdowns on the journey to Holman Clavel. Although taxing, the cyclist is rewarded by the truly magnificent scenery in these remote valleys.

From Holman Clavel the route passes through Pitminster and Corfe where the terrain is more gentle as the road winds its way through Orchard Pitman to the charming village of Stoke St Mary. The wooded hillsides are always in sight as the route continues through Thurlbear, Staple, Fitzpaine, Curland , Broadway and Ilminster.

This route is better suited to the experienced cyclist as there are steep climbs and steep descents.

Start: (O.S. Landranger sheet 193, Grid reference ST 362143)
Leave the car park in Shudrick Lane, Ilminster, and turn left at the junction with Ditton Street. Head away from the town for 1.3 miles along a sweeping right hand bend to the A358. Turn right and then take the first turning on the left to Crock Street (1mile) and Barley Hill (1.75 miles).

Points of interest
Ilminster: (see Ride 15).

Stage 1 Cork Street – Barley Hill – Sticklepath – Street Ash – Buckland St Mary
The road rises steadily from this junction and at the crossroads in Crock Street keep straight on to Sticklepath (1.5miles) and Buckland St Mary (2.5 miles) passing Haines Hill House on the left. The road continues up Barley Hill along a road overlooking a valley on the left. Keep straight on and at Sticklepath ignore the road to the left that descends into the valley and pass through this small hamlet to a crossroads. Join the road which is

diagonally opposite by turning right and then immediately left (the road sign is damaged).

The road continues to climb and at the next T-junction turn right and then almost immediately left. Follow the road to the next crossroads at the summit of the hill. Turn right towards Taunton and downhill past the Ash Street Nurseries to the A303(T). At the Give Way sign turn right and then immediately left to join the road to Buckland St Mary (1 mile). (The Eagle Tavern is situated nearby on the A303(T)). Take the next turn on the left and at the next crossroads continue directly across and into Buckland St Mary.

Points of interest

Buckland St. Mary: a small charming village in the Blackdown Hills.

Castle Neroche: in the Middle Ages this hill fort stood at the western end of Neroche Forest. The tree covered area is the site of a Norman castle once owned by William the Conqueror's half brother. The area is now managed by the Forestry Commission who have created a number of nature trails in the area.

Stage 2 Buckland St Mary – Blackwater – Buckland Farm – Holman Clavel

Turn sharp right round the church in Buckland St Mary with the school to the left and continue to the crossroads at Buckland Hill. Keep straight on round a right-hand bend to a T-junction. Turn left onto the Taunton road, continue past Beehive Farm on the left and bear left at the signpost to Blackwater.

The narrow road runs downhill to the bottom of the valley and climbs steeply through Blackwater. It then flattens out a little before reaching a junction with a road from the right. Turn left and ride for a short distance along the edge of Staple Common. Then take the first turn on the left along a narrow lane which runs along the rim of a valley and provides beautiful views in the direction of Buckland St Mary. Bear round to the right and at a crossroads pass directly across and continue along the rim of the valley. The road then descends steeply through trees to a brook at the bottom. There is then a short steep climb past Buckland Farm to the top of the hill at Westhay Farm, (on the right). The road then descends steeply into another valley and bears to the left. Disregard the road joining it from the right and continue to the next turn on the right. Climb the steep winding road to the B3170 and cross to join the road opposite. Turn right at the next T-junction which is a short distance away. Carry straight on across the crossroads at Holman Clavel passing the Holman Clavel Inn on the left.

Points of interest

Holman Clavel: in the Blackdowns where six lanes meet, indicating that it may have been an important meeting place. The Holman Clavel Inn is welcoming and strategically placed for the thirsty traveller. 'Holman' means made of holly and 'Clavel' is the name given to the beam which forms the mantel of the large fire places in old houses.

Stage 3 Holman Clavel – Blagdon Hill – Pitminster – Corfe – Stoke St Mary

Continue along the road from Holman Clavel to the next crossroads. Turn right towards Blagdon Hill (1.5 miles) and Taunton. There are beautiful views over the surrounding landscape as the tree-lined road winds its way along, before dropping down steeply round an S-bend into Blagdon Hill. Pass the Post Office on the left and at the fork in the road outside the village, take the right hand (signposted) road to Pitminster (0.5 miles) and Corfe (1.5 miles). The road takes a sharp right-hand bend into Pitminster past the Queens Arms public house and the church, both on the right. At the fork in the road bear right to Corfe (0.75 miles). Follow this road to the B3170 in Corfe and turn left. The White Hart stands nearby. The church of St Nicholas on the right of the road is worth a visit.

Leave Corfe and travel along the B3170 and take the first turn on the right. Pass Corfe Barton House on the right and follow the road as it bears sharp right and winds its way to Heale and then on to Orchard Portman. Pass through Orchard Portman and at the T-junction turn left and then take the first turn on the right at a difficult S-bend. Continue along this narrow road over Broughton Brook. At the next T-junction turn right to Stoke St Mary (0.25 miles). To tour the village turn left towards Henlade. This charming village and the church of St Mary are well worth visiting.

Points of interest

Corfe: a small pretty village situated at the foot of the Blackdown Hills, with interesting houses dating from the 16th century to the present.

Stoke St Mary: a charming village set beneath a backcloth of the wooded Stoke Hill.

Stage 4 Stoke St Mary – Staple Fitzpaine – Curland – Broadway – Ilminster

To continue the tour return to the Chapel and continue past the Half Moon to Thurlbear (0.75 miles). Turn right at the Greenway Farm and continue to Thurlbear. Pass the church on the left and the rectory on the right and follow the road as it bears sharply to the right to the T-junction in Netherclay. Turn left towards Staple Fitzpaine (1.75 miles) via Winter Wells and Badger Street. Pass through the crossroads in Staple Fitzpaine passing the church and almshouses on the right. Take the next turn on the left to Curland. At the triangle of land near the telephone box in Curland keep to the right and continue towards Bickenhall. Turn right at the next signpost to Broadway (3.0 miles) and Ilminster (5 miles). This is a long straight road. Continue to the signpost to Broadway at a crossroads. Turn left, pass the Bell Inn on the right, and turn right at the signpost to Ilminster along South View. The road crosses a stream and at the Give Way sign at Puddlebridge turn left down to the A358. Turn left and follow the road round the roundabout and then down to a second roundabout to pick up the road down into Ilminster and the car park.

Points of interest

Staple Fitzpaine: mentioned in the Domesday Book. The church of St. Peter dates from the 12th century and the Almshouse from the 17th. The manor house is near the church.

Curland: a path from this hamlet leads up through the woods to Castle Neroche.

Broadway: the name comes from 'broad way', an ancient path through the Forest of Neroche, between the Iron Age hill fort and Ham Hill. The 16th and 17th century houses are well preserved.

RIDE 17

FROM BRIDGWATER TO THE QUANTOCKS

Distance: 30 miles.
Journey time: (including a visit to the Coleridge Cottage in Nether Stowey) approximately 6-7 hours.

Route Description
This route begins in Bridgwater and explores two separate areas on the eastern slopes of the Quantock Hills before returning to Bridgwater. The initial stage of the tour passes through the town and on to Durleigh from where a gentle ascent is made to Enmore and Pightly. From here the route passes through Spaxton, Nether Stowey, Over Stowey, Aisholt and Bush before returning to Pightly to begin the second stage of the ride. The road up from Durleigh is rejoined and a steep ascent made to a point just below the summit of Broomfield Hill. From here the journey is downhill past Fyne Court, the village of Broomfield and down winding lanes to Goathurst, Durleigh and Bridgwater. Apart from the short journey along the A39 into Nether Stowey the journey from Durleigh is along minor roads and through a maze of narrow lanes.

The villages and hamlets offer much in terms of historical origins and folklore and in addition the views and the splendid isolation on some sections of the route keep the rider's interest throughout. The ride is a mixture of the gradients one might expect in such a terrain. The longest ascent is up Broomfield Hill and the descent where care has to be taken is the road down to Lower Aisholt. This is a splendid ride, with a number of places for refreshments on the route.

Start: (O.S. Landranger sheets 181 and 182, Grid reference for sheet 182 ST301371)
Turn left at the exit to the car park into Watson's Lane, Bridgwater, and follow the one-way system to Church Street. Turn right and then right again into the main street called Eastover. Continue to the bridge over the River Parrett. Cross the bridge and instead of cycling round the one way system walk through the pedestrian precinct in Fore Street and join the High Street near St Mary's Church. Ride along the High Street to the traffic lights at the junction with the Broadway. Pass directly through the traffic lights to join the Durleigh Road. Continue along this road to the outskirts of the town and turn left at the signpost to Bishops Lydeard and Taunton. Bear round to the right and follow the road as it runs parallel to the Durleigh reservoir.

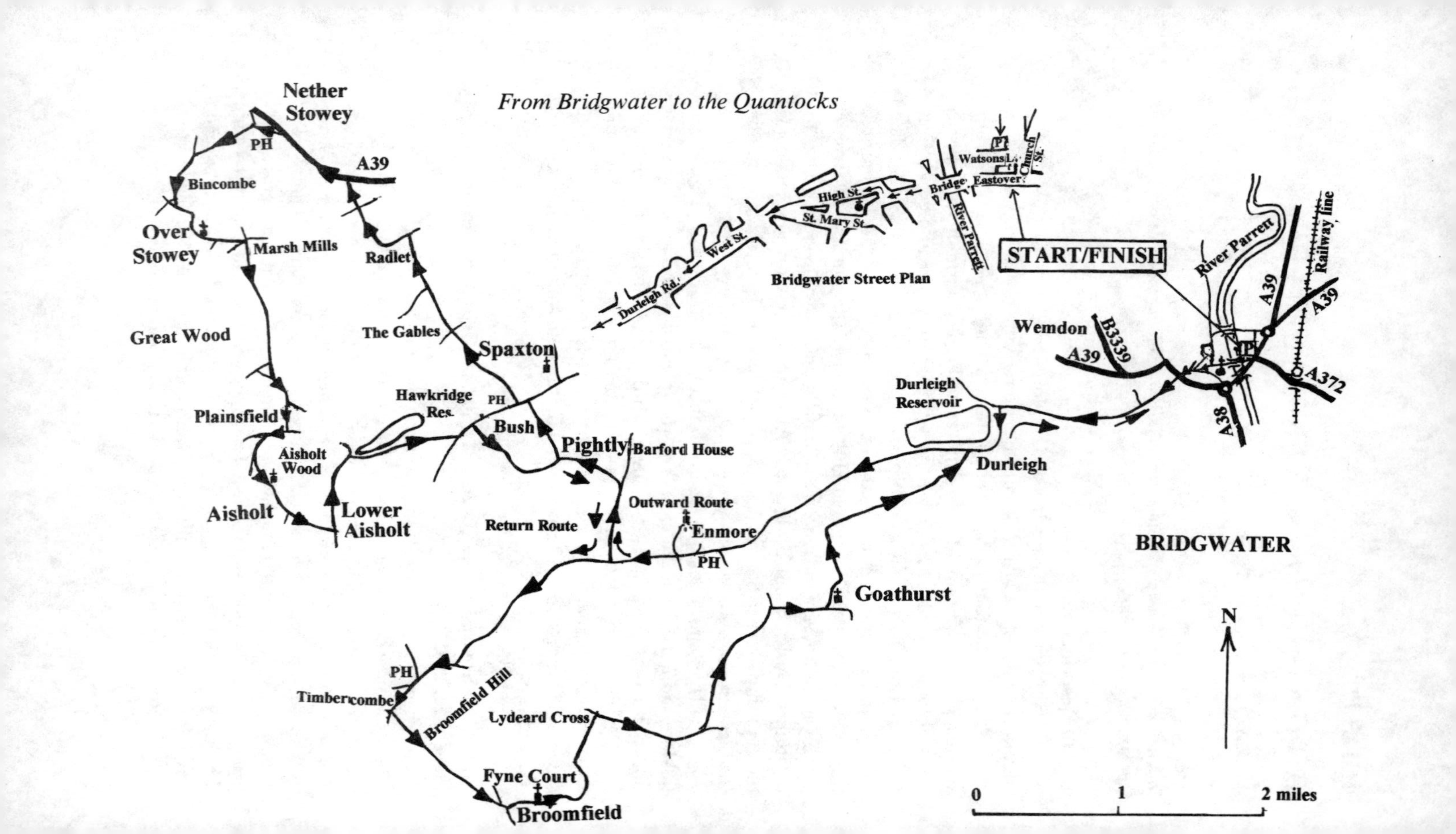
From Bridgwater to the Quantocks
Nether Stowey
PH
A39
Bincombe
Over Stowey
Marsh Mills
Radlet
Great Wood
The Gables
Spaxton
Hawkridge Res.
PH
Bush
Plainsfield
Aisholt Wood
Pightly
Barford House
Aisholt
Lower Aisholt
Outward Route
Return Route
Enmore
PH
Goathurst
PH
Timbercombe
Broomfield Hill
Lydeard Cross
Fyne Court
Broomfield
Watsons La.
Church St.
Bridge
Eastover
High St.
St. Mary St.
West St.
Durleigh Rd.
River Parrett
START/FINISH
Bridgwater Street Plan
River Parrett
Railway line
A39
A39
Wemdon
B3339
A39
A372
A38
Durleigh Reservoir
Durleigh
BRIDGWATER
N
0
1
2 miles

Points of interest

Bridgwater: a small industrial town on the tidal River Parrett. It was once a prosperous medieval port but little remains apart from the 14th century Church of St Mary, the street names and layout. A statue of the town's most famous son, Robert Blake, stands at the head of Fore Street.

Stage 1 Durleigh – Enmore – Pightly – Spaxton – Nether Stowey

Continue along the road passing the Tynte Arms on the left to a signpost to Barford Park and Spaxton (2 miles). Turn right and the church at Enmore can be seen down across the fields to the right. At the entrance to Barford Park take the road to Spaxton which bears to the left. The road eventually rises up a hill to a left-hand bend to Pightley. At the signpost at Bush Lane take the road to the right. At the next T-junction in Spaxton, turn left and then almost immediately right and follow the sign to Nether Stowey (3 miles). At the next T-junction in Radlet turn left and follow the signposted direction to Nether Stowey. At the Stop sign go straight ahead to join the A39. Turn left and continue to a signpost to Nether Stowey and turn left.

At the Clock Tower, in the village, the road to the right leads up to the Coleridge Cottage near the Ancient Mariner Public House.

Points of interest

Enmore: William the Conqueror gave the Manor to the Malet family until John Perceval purchased it and built a medieval castle on the site, the remains of which were incorporated into a Victorian building.

Spaxton: once associated with the woollen trade, its prosperity being reflected in the interesting old church and manor house.

Nether Stowey: the name means 'stone Way' an important route in Saxon times. It is a pleasant and attractive village with listed buildings and the remains of a moat and castle. The poet Coleridge lived in Lime Street; his house (NT) is open to the public.

Stage 2 Nether Stowey – Over Stowey – Aisholt – Lower Aishalt – Pightly

From the Clock Tower take the road along Castle Street to Over Stowey. The road rises out of the village and then falls steeply to a junction. Bear left and at a small triangular grassed area, turn left. Follow the road past the church in Over Stowey and continue to the crossroads. Turn right to Plainsfield passing Great Wood on the right. Continue along the S-bend in Plainsfield to where the road bears left and take the narrow (signposted) road on the right to Aisholt. At the next junction bear right and continue in a curving left-handed direction to where the road rises steeply to a fork. Take the left-hand road which descends to the bottom of the valley from where it rises, crosses a stream and enters Aisholt, with the church on the left. Pass up through the village and keep bearing left disregarding any road or track to the right. From the top of the climb out of the village the road drops down to Lower Aisholt. This road is steep and care has to be taken.

Turn left at the crossroads at Lower Aisholt and at the Hawkridge reservoir turn right. Continue on beyond the end of the reservoir to where a road comes in from the right. Keep to the left from here and take the next turn on the right along Bush Lane to Pightly.

Points of interest

Over Stowey: a quiet village, situated higher up the Quantocks than Nether Stowey. The church has a restored Burne-Jones window.

Aisholt: a village in the Quantocks. Magnificent views can be obtained from the hill behind the 15th century church.

Stage 3 Pightly – Fyne Court – Broomfield – Goathurst – Durleigh – Bridgwater

From Pightly return to the road from Durleigh. At the junction turn right and climb steadily for about 1.5 miles. It eventually descends past the Travellers Rest Public House and continues to a crossroads and the Pines Cafeteria.

At the crossroads turn left to Fyne Court. The road rises through woodland and then falls quite rapidly to another junction. Take the signposted road to Fyne Court and Broomfield. The entrance to Fyne Court is on the left. Continue into Broomfield. A sharp S-bend leads past the church and out of the village and down to a crossroads at Lydeard Cross. Turn right to Goathurst. Continue and at the fork in the road bear left to Bridgwater. Follow the signposts to Bridgwater which will lead past the church in Goatfield and on to Durleigh. Turn right at the junction with the Durleigh to Taunton road and retrace the initial journey back to the car park in Bridgwater.

Points of interest

Fyne Court (NT): the owner Andrew Cross (1784-1855) carried out early experiments in elecricity, supposedly inspiring Mary Shelley to write 'Frankenstein'. The main house was destroyed by fire in 1894 and only the outbuildings remain. Now the home of the Somerset Trust for Nature Conservation.

Goathurst: the village is dominated by the Tynte family who married into the Halswell family of Halswell House, a 17th century house built onto an earlier manor house whose gardens are open to the public.

RIDE 18

ALONG THE SLOPES OF THE QUANTOCK AND BRENDON HILLS

Distance: 24 miles.
Journey time: approximately 6 hours moderately easy riding.

Route Description

The journey begins in Williton, continues north to the coastline overlooking the Bristol Channel at Doniford and then climbs up to West Quantoxhead. From here the route heads down the valley linking Taunton with the coast, passing through the charming village of Bicknoller, on the lower slopes of the Quantocks. It then crosses the main road from Taunton to explore the valley bottom near the West Somerset Railway line. Using minor roads, a return is made to the slopes of the Quantocks at Crowcombe via the pivotal point of the whole route at Heddon Oak. A short steep climb is made from Crowcombe before continuing the journey to Triscombe.

From Triscombe the main road is crossed once more on the way to Lydeard St Lawrence, a small village at the foot of the Brendon Hills. The variety of scenery and terrain is maintained on the journey back to Williton through Stogumber, Vellow and Sampford Brett.

The views from all parts of the ride are superb and the red sandstone of the village houses contrast markedly with those of the Somerset levels and the Mendips. The ride is decidely modest in its demands and the only sections where cycling is difficult is the climb from Doniford to West Quantoxhead and the short steep climb from Crowcombe to a point higher up the hillside. There are a number of pleasant downhill runs, a favourite one being through the wood near Lydeard St Lawrence to a point near the railway line.

Start: (O.S.Landranger sheet 181, Grid reference ST075411)

From the car park in Williton turn right into the main street and bear left by the thatched building directly ahead. This road is part of the B3191. At the Masons Arms Inn leave the B3191 and take the right-hand signposted road to Doniford. Continue along this road passing under a railway bridge to a Give Way sign. Turn right.

The road passes over a small bridge and rises to a flat stretch which overlooks a holiday camp near the sea. It continues upwards for about 0.5 miles before reaching a flat section with a copse on the left. Follow the road to the A39 at West Quantoxhead. Cross the road directly to a signposted

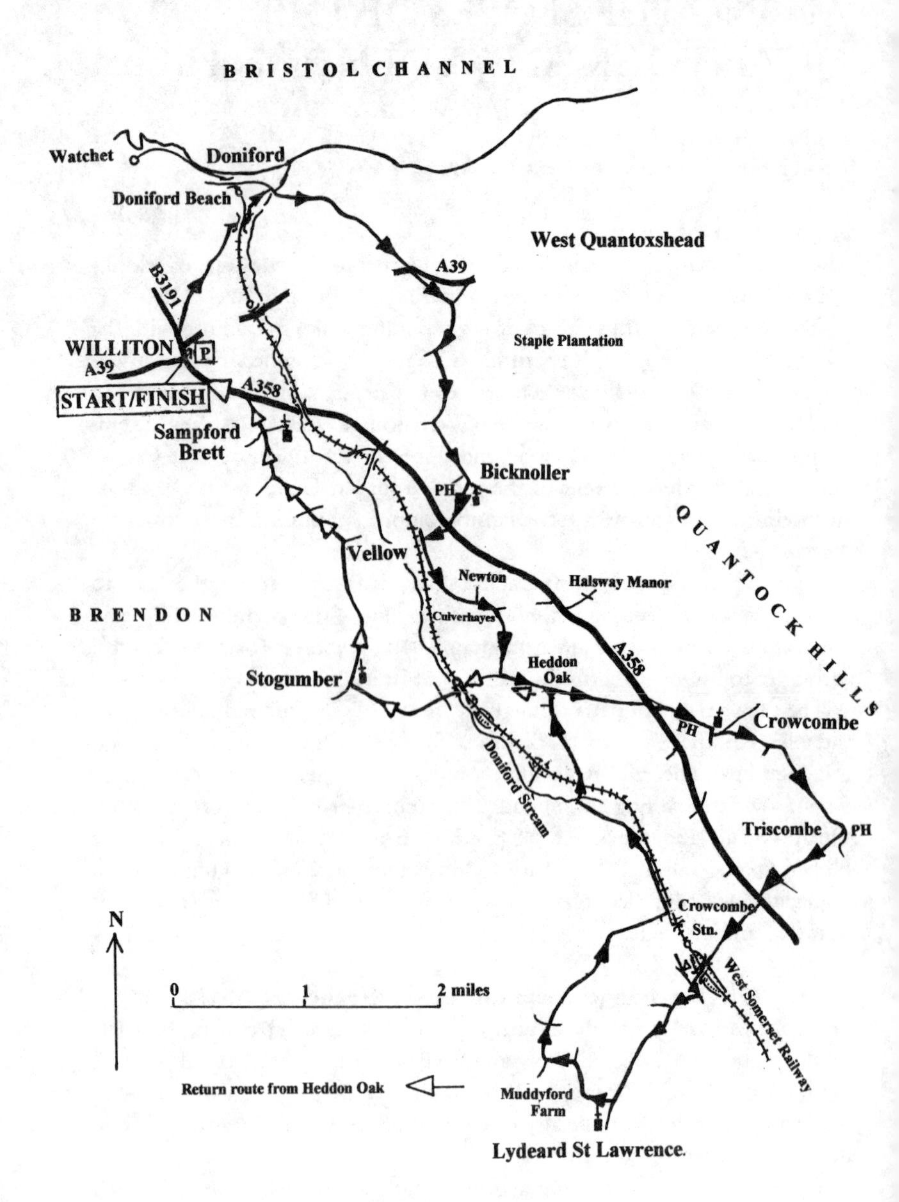
BRISTOL CHANNEL
Watchet
Doniford
Doniford Beach
West Quantoxshead
A39
B3191
WILLITON
P
A39
START/FINISH
A358
Staple Plantation
Sampford Brett
Bicknoller
PH
QUANTOCK HILLS
Vellow
Newton
Halsway Manor
BRENDON
Culverhayes
A358
Heddon Oak
Stogumber
PH
Crowcombe
Doniford Stream
Triscombe
PH
Crowcombe Stn.
N
0
1
2 miles
West Somerset Railway
Return route from Heddon Oak
Muddyford Farm
Lydeard St Lawrence.

road to Bicknoller (1.75 mile). Follow the road to a Give Way sign. Turn right (Weacombe Road) and continue to another signpost to Bicknoller (1 mile). Turn left along this narrow road to a third signpost and turn left again to Bicknoller along a road with high banks. In the village at a signpost near a small triangle of intersecting roads continue straight ahead down Trundle Lane which bears right round a corner and passes the church on the left. Pass the Bicknoller Inn and continue to the A358.

Points of interest

Williton: a pleasant town on the route to West Somerset. It is an excellent centre from which to explore the Quantock and Brendon Hills and the Somerset coast.

Bicknoller: lies on the slopes of the Quantock Hills, with fine views of the Brendon Hills. The Bicknoller Inn is an excellent place of refreshment for the thirsty traveller.

Stage 1 Bicknoller – Crowcombe – Triscombe

Turn left along the A358 and take the next turn on the right, to Newton (0.5 miles). The road runs towards the railway and bears left before running parallel to it as far as the next signpost. Follow the road through Culverhayes and at the next unsignposted junction disregard the road from Newton on the left, and carry straight on to the next signpost. Turn right turn towards Stogumber. This little used road leads down to a brook before rising up to a signpost. Turn left to Crowcombe (1.75 miles) passing a farm with a clock tower on the right before reaching a junction called Heddon Oak. Continue to the A358. The tour comes back to this point on the return journey to Williton.

Cross the A358 into Crowcombe passing the Carew Arms on the right, the old market cross on the left and on to the Church of the Holy Ghost next to Crowcombe Court.

From the church ride the short distance to a junction and turn left towards Over Stowey. Follow this steep road and take the first turn on the right to Triscombe (1.25 miles). The road rises for 0.5 miles and levels out at Little Quantock Farm. Disregard the right turn just short of the farm and continue along a roller coaster route to Triscombe and the Blue Ball Inn.

Points of interest

Heddon Oak: a gallows tree from which a number of the Duke of Monmouth followers were hanged after judgement by Judge Jeffreys.

Crowcombe: stands on the south-western slopes of the Quantocks and is regarded as the most charming village in the area. The church is built of red sandstone, the tower dating from the 14th century. Of the many features of the church perhaps the most interesting are the Elizabethan bench ends. Other points of interest include the medieval market cross, the churchyard cross, the Church House and the view of Crowcombe Court.

Stage 2 Triscombe – Lydeard St Lawrence – Stogumber – Vellow

From the Blue Ball Inn ride to the A358. Turn left and then first right to Lydeard St. Lawrence (no signpost). Continue along this tree-lined road over the railway and past the Youth Hostel to a junction. Turn left to Lydeard St Lawrence (1 mile) and bear right to a fork. Take the left-hand road to Lydeard St Lawrence (no village nameplate). In the village take the first turn on the right to Westowe bearing right by Muddyford Farm, down a steep hill past Westowe Manor Farm on the right. Continue uphill to a T-junction. Turn right towards Crowcombe station and go straight ahead at the next crossroads and down through a wood to a signpost near the railway line.Turn left to Stogumber (3.5 miles) along this rather rough road to a crossing point. Do not cross the railway line but continue straight on with Roebuck Farm on the opposite side of the railway. Continue uphill to a signpost.

Take the road to Heddon Oak and Stogumber (2.75 miles). If clear cross the railway line and continue the journey to Heddon Oak. From here the road to Stogumber passes under the railway line near the station. Follow the signpost to Stogumber (0.75 miles), and through the village to a T-junction near Sawpits Close. Turn right towards Vellow.

Points of interest

Lydeard St Lawrence: a farming community situated at the foot of the Brendon Hills with a red sandstone church.

Stogumber: a large picturesque farming village on the lower slopes of the Brendon Hills.

Stage 3 Vellow – Sampford Brett – Williton

There is sharp right-hand bend at the entrance to Vellow with an un-signposted minor road leading uphill out of the village.Take this road to Sampford Brett. At the next crossroads take the unsignposted road straight ahead to Sampford Brett instead of the signposted direction to the right. Continue along this road, through the village to the A358 on the outskirts of Williton where you can return to the car park. (This alternative route through Vellow and Sampford Brett avoids joining the A358 too soon and the journey is free of traffic until Williton is reached.)

RIDE 19

A TOUR FROM WELLINGTON

Distance: 23 miles.
Journey time: (including the visit to the Wellington Monument) approximately 5 hours.

Route Description
The town of Wellington stands at the southern edge of the Vale of Taunton and at the foot of the Blackdown Hills, a position which is ideally suited as a centre for a tour of the Vale of Taunton and the steep-tree lined escarpment and high ridge of the Blackdown Hills.

From Wellington the route heads in a westerly direction to Sampford Arundel and then north to Greenham before continuing to Thorne St Margaret. After crossing the River Tone the ride follows a curving path through Langford Budeville to Nynehead, before recrossing the River Tone between East Nynehead and Bradford-on-Tone. The relatively flat terrain of the Vale is left behind shortly after leaving West Buckland when the steep climb to the ridge of the Blackdown Hills begins. The Wellington Monument, a prominent landmark, stands proud at the western end of the ridge and is worth a visit. The road near this high point descends steeply to Rockwell and Wellington.

The journey is one of contrasts, the first half being of little used lanes, well tended farmland and graceful villages, the riding being relatively easy. The second half begins with a stiff climb where the rider may have to dismount. Take this opportunity to admire the superb views over the Vale of Taunton, the Quantocks and the Brendon Hills.

Start: (O.S.Landranger sheet 181, Grid reference ST141206)
The start and finish point for this tour is the car park in Longforth Road, Wellington. Turn right from the car park into Longforth Road and turn right at the traffic lights at the High Street. Continue along this main street, through the traffic lights and out of the town towards Rockwell Green. At the next traffic lights in Rockwell Green, continue directly ahead passing the church and a tall water tower on the right. Take the first turning on the left to Sampford Moor and at the A38 keep straight on. At the next crossroads, at Pleamore Cross, continue straight ahead and take the first turn on the right to Sampford Arundel.

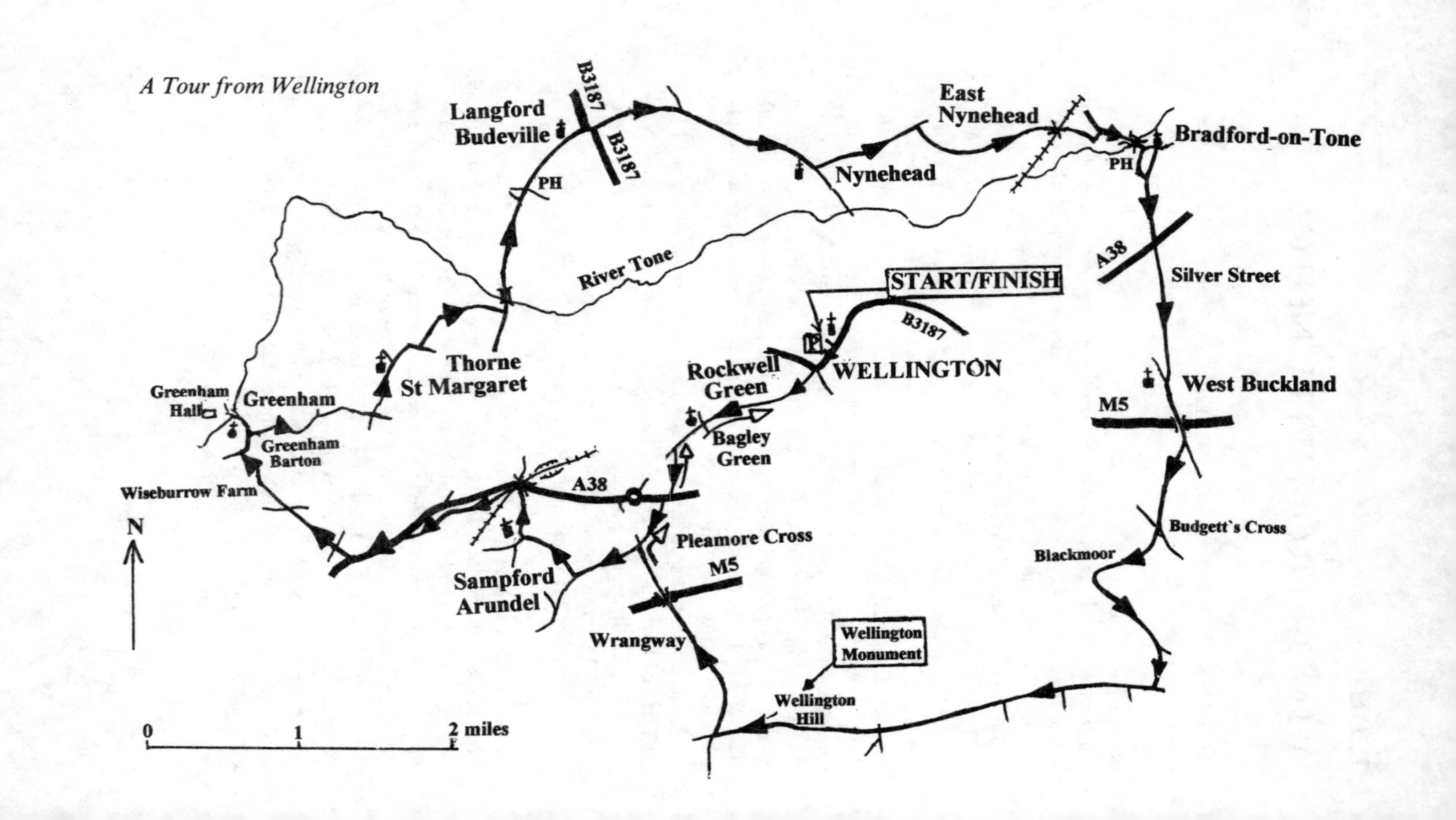
A Tour from Wellington
Langford
Budeville
B3187
B3187
PH
East
Nynehead
Nynehead
Bradford-on-Tone
PH
River Tone
A38
Silver Street
START/FINISH
B3187
P
WELLINGTON
Thorne
St Margaret
Rockwell
Green
West Buckland
M5
Greenham
Hall
Greenham
Greenham
Barton
Bagley
Green
Wiseburrow Farm
A38
N
Pleamore Cross
Budgett's Cross
Blackmoor
M5
Sampford
Arundel
Wrangway
Wellington
Monument
Wellington
Hill
0
1
2 miles

Stage 1 Sampford Arundel – Greenham – Thorne St Margaret – Langford Budville – Nynehead

The road runs downhill into the village, past the church and down a lane to Beam Bridge. Pass under the railway line and turn immediately left along a minor road which runs parallel to but distant from the A38. Continue to the A38. Turn left and take the first turn on the right towards Greenham. This road passes through two crossroads and runs along the Somerset/Devon border passing Wiseburrow Farm. On the hill to the left stands Greenham Hall. At the bottom of the hill, instead of bearing left into the village, turn right up the lane passing Greenham Barton on the left. Continue up round a sharp left-hand bend keeping to the right at the signpost to Thorne St Margaret. Climb to the top of the hill from where there is a clear view of the Wellington Monument. Just over the summit turn left at the crossroads and travel into Thorne St. Margaret (1 mile).

The road runs down to the River Tone. Cross the bridge and continue uphill past Bere Farm to a triangular junction. Follow the road to the right into Langford Budville. The Martlet Inn is on the right and St Peters Church directly ahead. Pass through the village to a Give Way sign. Turn right towards Wellington on the B3187 and turn left down a little used lane towards Nynehead. This is a very pleasant part of the ride. The road passes through the hamlet of Hayward before bearing left past the church and Nynehead Court.

Points of interest

Sampford Arundel: an old Saxon settlement. The church contains a unique medieval sculpture of hands holding a heart above a holy water stoop.

Thorne St Margaret: picturesque village with a small, 800 year old church and a Saxon font.

Nynehead: an attractive village whose church houses some 15th century Italian sculptures and some fine monuments.

Stage 2 Nynehead – East Nynehead – Bradford-on-Tone – West Buckland

Follow the road through Nynehead towards East Nynehead. Do not deviate until a signpost to East Nynehead is reached. Pass through the village to a railway crossing with automatic barriers and on to a T-junction near the River Tone. Turn right, cross the bridge and climb the hill into Bradford-on-Tone. The White Horse Inn is on the right. From the church on the left continue to West Buckland. At the A38 cross the road directly and proceed down Silver Street with the Grange Restaurant on the left. Disregard the first road on the left and follow the road into West Buckland.

Points of interest

Bradford-on-Tone: 15th century bridge over the River Tone.

West Buckland: St Mary's Church stands high overlooking the surrounding countryside and can be seen floodlit at night from the M5 motorway. It contains a Norman font and 15th century carvings.

Stage 3 West Buckland – Wellington Monument – Wrangway – Rockwell Green – Wellington

From West Buckland the road passes over the M5 and at the signpost bear right towards Blackmoor. At the next junction (Budgett's Cross) keep straight on. This is the bottom of the escarpment which leads to the ridge. The initial climb is gradual but quickly steepens to give outstanding views over the Vale of Taunton, the Quantocks and the Brendon Hills. Near the top the road bears to the right to a junction with the ridge road. Turn right and ride for about 2 miles to the entry to the Wellington Monument. The track to the site is not smooth but presents no real problem. On returning rejoin the road, turn right and follow the road down Wellington Hill below the monument, at this western limit of the Blackdown Hills, and on to Wrangway. From Wrangway the road crosses the M5 to Pleamore Cross, across the A38 to Rockwell Green and back into Wellington.

RIDE 20

A TOUR THROUGH THE VALE OF TAUNTON

Distance: 34 miles.
Journey time: approximately 6-7 hours.

Route Description

This ride explores the Vale of Taunton, which lies between the Quantock, the Brendon and the Blackdown Hills. The tour begins in Taunton and speedily leaves the town for the quiet and remote lanes through the villages of Fulford, Cushuish, Toulton and Cothelstone before turning to Bishops Lydeard. Crossing the valley to Halse and Milverton provides wonderful views of the Quantocks and a distinct change of architectural styles. From just outside Milverton the ride joins a remote lane that leads past the Quaking House and down a memorable descent to the B3187. This is followed by a steady climb from Croford to Fitzhead.

A long run down the valley from Fitzhead to the river crossing near Tarr, and the subsequent climb up and over the hill to meet the B3224 at Handy Cross, maintains the element of surprise that occurs continuously on this route. The ride along the B3224 is minimised by using a little used lane for the descent to Combe Florey, a village of great charm. The journey from Combe Florey to West Bagborough, an attractive but long straggling village, forms part of the route to the ridge on the summit of the Quantock Hills. Along this ridge there are excellent views all the way to Broomfield. The steep descent to Kingstone St Mary provides a final view over the Vale of Taunton before the return to Taunton. The ride has a balanced number of descents and climbs and is well within the capabilities of a regular cyclist.

Start: (O.S. Landranger sheets 181,182, 193, Grid reference for sheet 193 ST226254)

Turn left at the exit to the public car park near Taunton railway station and at the junction with Cheddon Road move to the furthest lane of this two lane one-way system. Pass through the traffic lights and at the next traffic lights near the Oak and Acorn public house keep straight on.

Stage 1 Fulford – Cushuish – Cothelstone – Bishops Lydeard

Follow the road towards Kingstone St Mary. Pass the Cottage Inn on the left and continue to the crossroads near the 30 mph speed limit sign outside Kingstone St Mary. Turn left down Parsonage Lane passing Parsonage Farm on the right. At the next signpost follow the road left and then right

A Tour through the Vale of Taunton

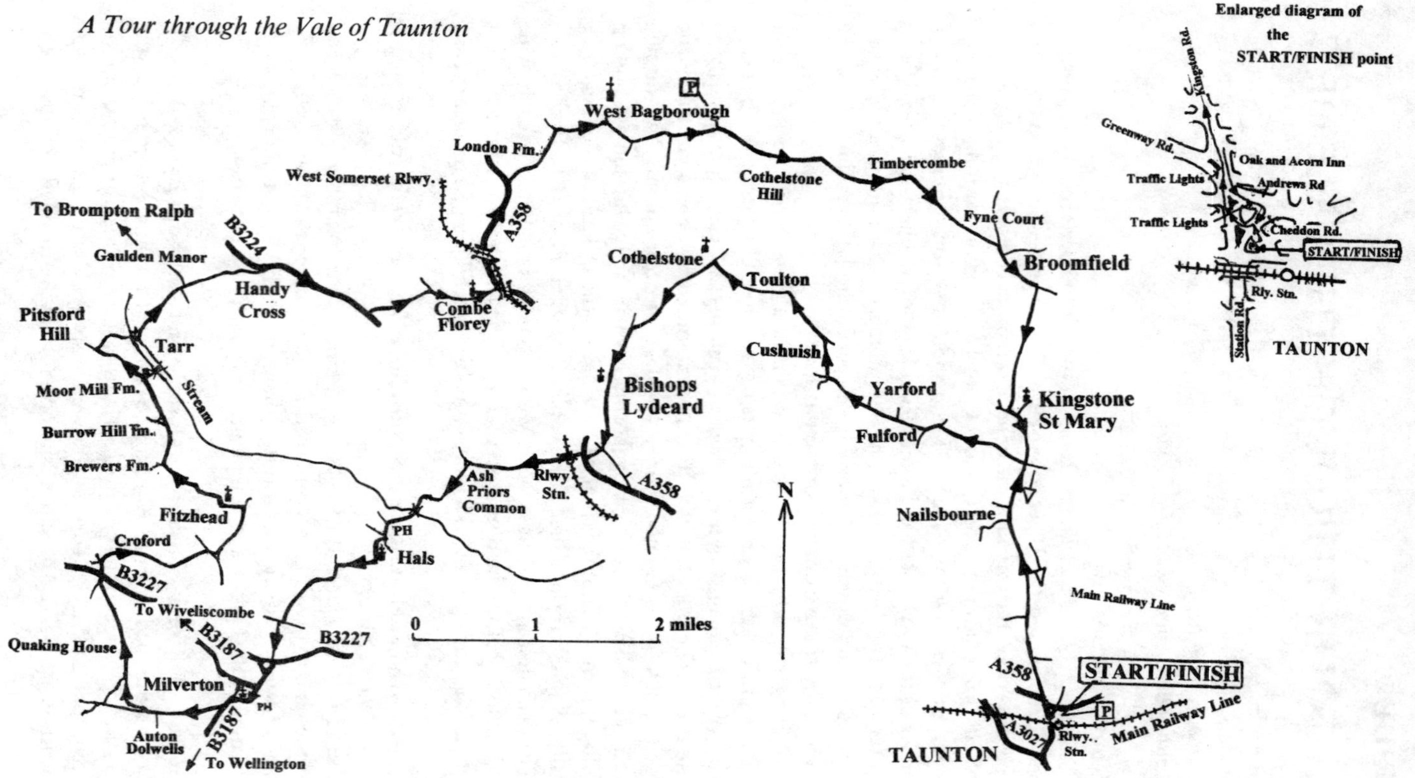

West Bagborough
P
London Fm.
West Somerset Rlwy.
A358
Cothelstone Hill
Timbercombe
Fyne Court
Broomfield
To Brompton Ralph
B3224
Gaulden Manor
Handy Cross
Combe Florey
Cothelstone
Toulton
Pitsford Hill
Tarr
Cushuish
Moor Mill Fm.
Stream
Bishops Lydeard
Yarford
Kingstone St Mary
Burrow Hill Fm.
Fulford
Brewers Fm.
Ash Priors Common
Rlwy Stn.
A358
N
Fitzhead
PH
Nailsbourne
Croford
Hals
B3227
To Wiveliscombe
0
1
2 miles
Main Railway Line
B3187
B3227
Quaking House
Milverton
A358
START/FINISH
PH
P
B3187
Main Railway Line
Auton Dolwells
A3027
Rlwy. Stn.
To Wellington
TAUNTON

Enlarged diagram of the START/FINISH point

Kingston Rd.
Greenway Rd.
Oak and Acorn Inn
Traffic Lights
Andrews Rd
Traffic Lights
Cheddon Rd.
START/FINISH
Rly. Stn.
Station Rd.
TAUNTON

to Bishops Lydeard (3.0 miles), passing through Fulford and Yarford to another crossroads and signpost. Turn right to Cushuish and at a T-junction near a farm turn left and follow the road down to an S-bend into Toulton. The road then passes through a farmyard and down a fenced drive from which Cothelstone church and the gateway to Cothelstone Manor can be seen. Turn left at the T-junction at the end of the fenced drive, and ride down into Bishops Lydeard (1.25 miles). Carry straight on through the village passing the Gardeners Arms and the Almshouses, both on the left, to the A358.

Points of interest

Taunton: the county town, and of considerable importance as a market town, with many fine buildings, including a Norman castle (which contains the County Museum).

Cothelstone: a small village of cottages and a 12th century church behind the Manor House, the home of the Stawell family. The impressive gateway to the manor was the site of the hanging of two Monmouth rebels condemned by Judge Jeffreys.

Bishops Lydeard: a pleasant village at the foot of the Quantock Hills with a striking red sandstone church tower. There are also restored 16th century almshouses.

Stage 2 Bishops Lydeard – Halse – Milverton

Turn right onto the A358 and then almost immediately left to Ash Priors (1 mile), Halse (2 miles) and Milverton (4 miles). Cross the bridge over the West Somerset Railway line at the Bishops Lydeard station and follow the road to Ash Priors Common. This is a large open space and at the fork bear left to Halse (1 mile) and Milverton (3 miles). The road winds its way towards Halse and bears sharp left by the New Inn as it enters the main street. Continue through the village and take the second turn on the right to Milverton.

The road rises steeply for a short distance and then bears left round a corner passing the church over to the left. Continue to a T-junction. Turn left and follow the winding lane which rises steeply to a crossroads at the summit. Turn right and then immediately left to the road to Milverton which can be seen clearly from this high point. The road drops steeply to the B3227. Turn right and then bear left to a roundabout and bear left again to Milverton. Cross the river bridge and cycle up the hill. Disregard the sign to Wiveliscombe and continue up Silver Street which becomes Fore Street (part of the B3187 to Wellington) near the Globe Inn. Ride up Fore Street, and at the sharp bend bear left with the B3187. Take the first turn on the right, pass the school, and continue up this road until outside the village.

Take the first turn to the right (just beyond the turn on the left to Auton

Dolwells). At first sight this narrow lane appears to be a rough track but the surface improves further on. It passes a Friends' Quaking House on the left, with a cemetery dated 1681. The road then descends for 0.75 miles, passing through wood to the B3227.

Points of interest

Halse: an attractive village in a fine setting, with houses fronting the street. The 12th century church has a magnificent screen.

Milverton: possibly a Saxon market town. The Georgian houses are the result of the growth of the woollen industry in the 18th century. Thomas Young (1773-1829), a famous resident, developed the wave theory of light and researched into the structure and working of the eye.

Stage 3 Croford – Fitzhead – Handy Cross – Combe Florey

At the B3227 turn left and then immediately right to Croford (0.5 miles) and Fitzhead (2 miles). The road bears right past Hill Acre Farm, through the village and up a steep wooded hill. The road then descends to a T-junction. Turn right and at the signpost on the triangle of land, turn left to Fitzhead (0.75 miles). Follow the road to a left turn into the village.

Turn sharp right past the Tythe Barn near the church, and follow the winding road keeping to the right at all times. Bear right at the track to Brewers Farm. The road falls steeply and at the fork near Burrow Hill Farm take the right turn down into the valley. Ignore the turn to Tarr near Moor Mill Farm and continue towards Pitsford Hill. The road climbs up the side of the valley and at the next signpost turn right towards Lydeard St Lawrence. The road drops sharply to the bottom of the valley. Cross over the stream and pass a chapel on the left. At the road junction bear to the left (to Taunton and Lydeard St Lawrence) and climb up past Lower Tarr Farm (on the right) to the top of the hill. At the next signpost continue towards Bishops Lydeard and Taunton. (A visit to Gaulden Manor can be made at this point by taking the road to Brompton Ralph.) The road continues to the B3224. Turn right passing the Friendship Inn on the left. Pass the turn to Pyleigh on the right and continue along this tree-lined road to the next unsignposted turning on the left near the end of the wood. Turn left here off the B3224 and pass down through a wood to a T-junction. Turn right and ride into Combe Florey.

Points of interest

Combe Florey: an attractive village set in a wooded valley. The gatehouse is all that remains of the medieval manor. The village's residents have included the Reverend Sidney Smith, Terence Rattigan the playwright, and Evelyn Waugh the writer.

Stage 4 Combe Florey – West Bagborough – Fyne Court – Broomfield

Ride through the village, past the church and the gateway to the manor house, to the A358. Turn left along this busy road past the Farmers Arms on the left then under the West Somerset Railway bridge. The road makes a long sweeping right-hand bend followed by a sharp left-hand bend. Turn right to West Bagborough just round this bend, watching out for the traffic.

Follow the road through this long straggling village passing the church and cricket ground on the left. The road climbs to a T-junction on the summit ridge of the Quantocks. Keep right towards Taunton and at the next junction below Cothelstone Hill bear left towards Enmore and Bridgwater. The road runs downhill to a junction of five roads. Turn left and then immediately right to join the road to Broomfield and Fynne Court.

Follow the road to a point where it is joined by a road from the left. Carry straight on past the next turn on the left which leads to Fyne Court and the village of Broomfield. Take the first turn on the right at a triangular area of grass, to Kingstone St Mary. This lane leads to a stepped descent to Kingstone St Mary with impressive views over the Vale of Taunton. Turn left at the road junction in the village and follow the road to the traffic lights near the Oak and Acorn public house in Taunton. Pass through the lights and move to the right hand filter lane in order to turn right at the next set of lights into Cheddon Road and the car park.

Points of interest

Fyne Court (NT): (see Ride 17).

West Bagborough: a straggling village as in the 14th century the population built cottages half a mile away to escape the Black Death. Some of these still remain, as does the inn, The Rising Sun.

Kingstone St Mary: this once self-sufficient village is situated in a cider making area. The 15th century red sandstone tower of the church is of particular architectural interest as are the bench ends.

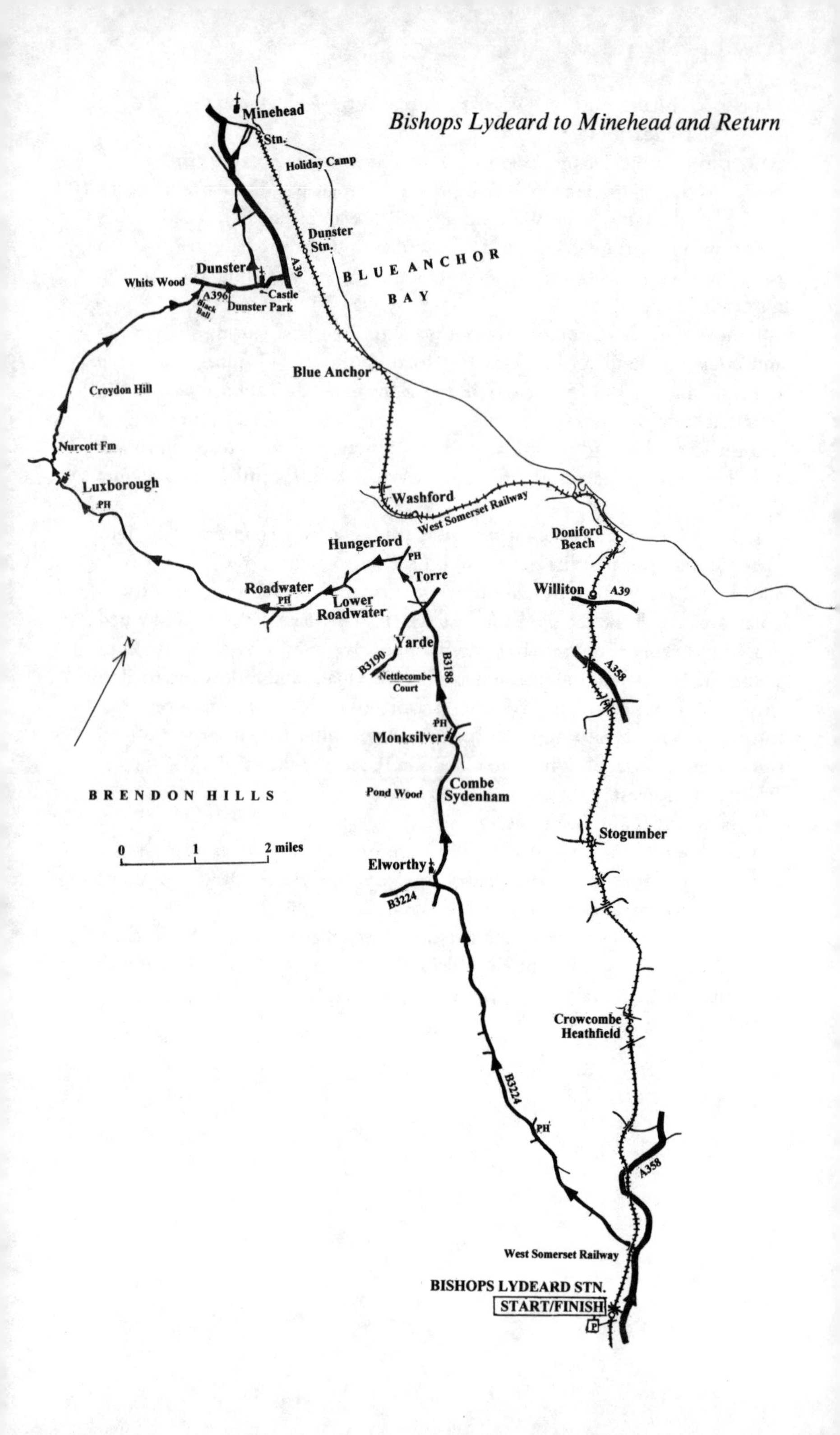
Bishops Lydeard to Minehead and Return
Minehead
Stn.
Holiday Camp
Dunster
Stn.
BLUE ANCHOR
BAY
A39
Dunster
Whits Wood
A396
Black Ball
Castle
Dunster Park
Blue Anchor
Croydon Hill
Nurcott Fm
Luxborough
PH
Washford
West Somerset Railway
Doniford
Beach
Hungerford
PH
Torre
Roadwater
PH
Lower
Roadwater
Williton
A39
N
Yarde
B3190
Nettlecombe
Court
B3188
A358
PH
Monksilver
BRENDON HILLS
Pond Wood
Combe
Sydenham
Stogumber
0
1
2 miles
Elworthy
B3224
Crowcombe
Heathfield
B3224
PH
A358
West Somerset Railway
BISHOPS LYDEARD STN.
START/FINISH
P

RIDE 21

BISHOPS LYDEARD TO MINEHEAD AND RETURN

(journey by road and rail)

Distance: 25 miles by road.
Journey time: approximately 6 hours by road.
Return by steam train: 1 hour 20 minutes.

Route Description

This is a cycle ride with a difference. It leaves from the car park of the West Somerset Railway station at Bishops Lydeard (5 miles outside Taunton on the A358) and makes its way up and over the Brendon Hills to Minehead. The return to Bishops Lydeard is a delightful journey by steam or diesel train from Minehead Station.

The ride passes through a lovely part of Somerset as it climbs steadily up to Elworthy, Combe Sydenham and Monksilver, before beginning a long valley ride to Luxborough. The ascent from the village to the summit of Croyden Hill is rewarded by wonderful panoramic views towards Dunkery Beacon and Selworthy Beacon whilst the long steep descent to Dunster and Minehead is a satisfying end to a most enjoyable and varied ride.

The return journey by rail follows the coastline to Blue Anchor and then travels inland to Washford before returning to the coast at Watchet. The final stage of the journey is along the valley separating the Quantock and Brendon hills. It is also possible to take an early train from Minehead to Bishops Lydeard and reverse the route.

For rail enquiries please telephone Minehead (0643) 704996 or the 24-hour Talking Timetable (0643) 707650.

Start: (O.S. Landranger sheet 181, Grid reference ST163290)

Leave the car park at Bishops Lydeard railway station and turn right onto the road coming from the left over the railway bridge. Continue to the A358 and turn left. The road winds along the valley with the church of Bishops Lydeard to the right and the railway line to the left. Take the left turn onto the B3224 signposted to Monksilver, pass under the railway bridge and the entrance to Ash Priors hospital on the left.

Points of interest

Bishops Lydeard: a pleasant village at the foot of the Quantock Hills with a striking red sandstone church tower and restored 16th century almshouses. The village and the railway station are separated by the A358 Taunton-Williton road.

Stage 1 Ash Priors Hospital – Elworthy – Combe Sydenham – Monksilver

Keep on the B3224 for 6 miles before reaching a Give Way sign at a crossroads. Turn right onto the B3188 to Elworthy. The road narrows, runs between high hedges and round a sharp S-bend and down to the bottom of the valley. There are a series of ponds along the bottom of the valley, which form part of the Combe Sydenham Country Park. Pass Combe Sydenham House and continue to Monksilver.

Points of interest

Combe Sydenham House: built in 1367. Elizabeth Sydenham, Francis Drake's second wife lived here.

Monksilver: an attractive village in the Brendon foothills.

Stage 2 Monksilver – Roadwater – Luxborough

Pass through Monksilver with the church and the Notely Arms on the left and remain on the B3188. Pass the turn on the left to Nettlecombe Court and continue up to a crossroads. Go directly across the B3190 to a minor road which bears round to the left by a house on the right. Follow the road downhill passing the Torre Fruit Farm and on to the White Horse Inn. Turn sharp left immediately after the White Horse Inn and follow the road to Roadwater and Luxborough. The road runs behind the Inn and down the wooded valley with a stream to the left. This is ideal for cycling.

Cycle through the village of Roadwater past the cricket ground on the left and the Valiant Soldier public house on the right. At the next signpost turn right to Luxborough (3.75 miles). Continue with the stream on the right into Luxborough. Turn right at the Royal Oak of Luxborough Inn. The road rises very steeply round an S- bend behind the inn, and continues rising to a summit. It then falls in a series of steps bearing right by a farm before rising to a sharp left turn below the church.The road dips down to Churchtown before climbing to a small triangle of land and a signpost. Turn right to Minehead (6.75miles).

Points of interest

Nettlecombe Court: the manor owned by the son of King Harold was seized by William the Conqueror. The great hall dates from 1599 and contains an organ built in 1666. Today the Court is leased to the Field Studies Council.

Luxborough: high up in the Brendon Hills with wonderful views.

Stage 3 Churchtown – Dunster – Minehead

Follow the road as it bears to the left and becomes little more than a narrow lane. It then winds downhill passing Nurcott Farm. The scenery and distant views are quite exceptional as the narrow lane rises to the top of Croydon Hill. Across the valley to the west there is Dunkery Hill and Dunkery Beacon and to the north-west Selworthy Beacon. The road descends very steeply to the valley bottom and the River Avill. Care must be taken on this descent. Continue through Whits Wood and along the edge of Black Ball Wood to the A396. Turn right and continue to the outskirts of Dunster. Just before the traffic lights near the church turn left up St George Street, a minor road which bypasses the main village and avoids riding along the busy A39 into Minehead. The road passes a school on the left and rises, passing a cross on the right.

At the next junction bear left (Combeland Road) and follow the road to the outskirts of Minehead down Church Street to the A39. Turn left and at the mini-roundabout bear right down Alcombe Road and right again down Ponsford Road. Continue along Tregonwell Road to The Avenue, the main street. Turn right to the Railway Station.

Points of interest

Dunster: is more a town than a village and its many attractions include the Castle, the main street, the Yarn Market and the church.

Minehead: a popular and pleasant seaside resort, with quaint cottages and passageways nestling around the 14th century church of St Michael on North Hill. It expanded as a resort with the coming of the railway in 1874. The latter was closed in 1971 and reopened as the West Somerset Railway, a private railway, in 1976. It now operates a service between Minehead and Bishops Lydeard, near Taunton, during the summer months. Timetable details can be obtained from the Tourist Informatiom Bureau in Minehead or by telephoning the 24-hour talking timetable on (0643) 707650.

A Short Ride from Watchet

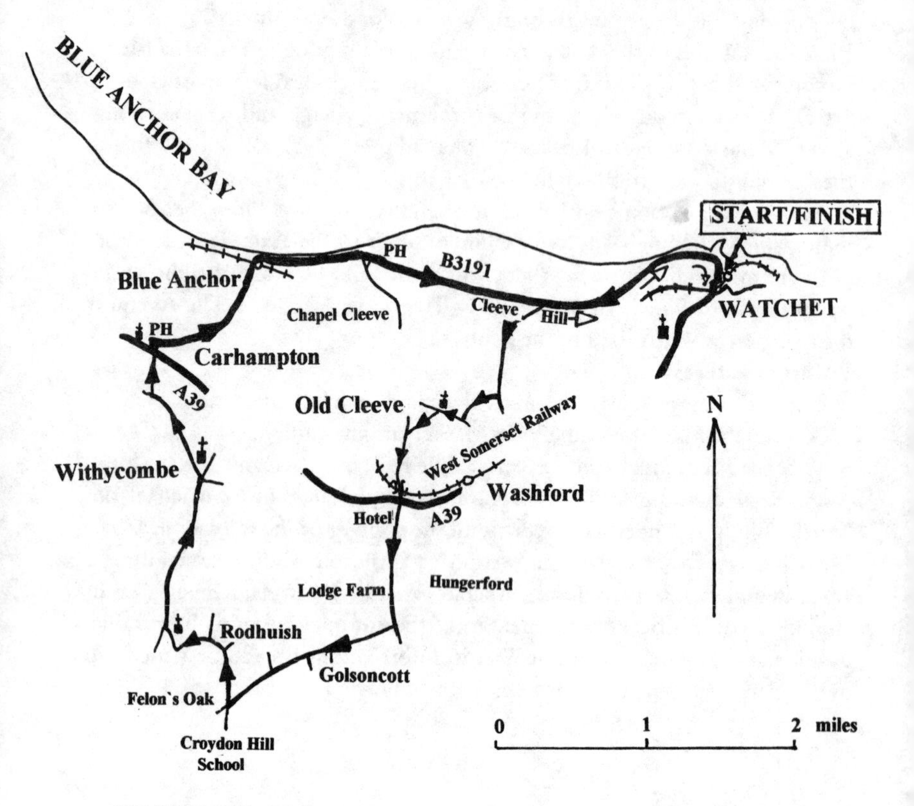

RIDE 22

A SHORT RIDE FROM WATCHET

Distance: 14 miles.
Journey time: approximately 3-4 hours.

Route Description
This is a short ride which takes the rider from the sea coast through the delightful village of Old Cleeve before climbing through quiet lanes to the splendid vantage points of the Brendon Hills.

From these high hills there are views of Dunster, Minehead and Exmoor to the north-west, a further expanse of the Brendon Hills to the south and a sizeable section of the coast along the Bristol Channel to the north. The return journey to Watchet is through Carhampton, Blue Anchor and over Cleeve Hill.

Start: (O.S. Landranger sheet 181, Grid reference ST071432)
Leave the exit to the car park near the railway station in Watchet, and turn right into Harbour Road. Turn right at Swain Street (B3191), the main road through the town, and at the Esplanade bear left along Market Street. Continue on to West Street and to the top of Cleeve Hill. After the summit take the first signposted left turn to Old Cleeve (1.5 miles).

Stage 1 Old Cleeve – Felon's Oak – Rodhuish – Withycombe
The road runs downhill to a signpost to Old Cleeve. Turn right and right again to the village. Take the road to the left at the junction near the church and ride through the village. At the next junction take the left-hand road passing over the railway bridge and to the A39, the main road to Minehead. Cross the A39 to join the road directly opposite, disregarding the sign 'Except for Access'. Continue on and bear right by the Honeypot Stud climbing up past Lodge Rocks Cottage on the left.

Turn right at the signpost to Rodhuish (2 miles) and continue climbing to the top. There are beautiful views to the right and left. At the first turn on the right (signposted to Rodhuish), continue straight ahead to Felon's Oak (0.5 miles), an alternate route to Rodhuish. Felon's Oak is identified by the sharp right-hand turn near the entrance gates to Croydon Hill School. Turn sharp right down the steep hill to Rodhuish. Pass through the hamlet and keep straight on at the small triangle of land with the tree commemorating the Festival of Britain. Pass the telephone box on the left, turn sharply to the right and up past the small white painted church of St Bartholomew.

At the next junction bear right, and where the road forks at the church in Withycombe, bear left to the A39.

Points of interest

Old Cleeve: a small picturesque village.

Stage 2 Carhampton – Blue Anchor – Watchet

Cross the A39 directly to join the B3191 and follow this road to Blue Anchor. It rises to the ridge overlooking the sea before dropping into Blue Anchor along Grove Road. Continue over the West Somerset Railway line near the signal box and along the sea front. At the end of the seafront bear right uphill passing the Blue Anchor Inn on the left. At the point where the road divides take the road to Watchet and climb to the top of Cleeve Hill, from where there are views of the Quantock and Brendon Hills and the coastline of the Bristol Channel. Continue along the B3191 into Watchet and back to the car park.

Points of interest

Blue Anchor: a popular seaside resort.

RIDE 23

A CIRCULAR TOUR FROM WIVELISCOMBE TO WIMBLEBALL LAKE

Distance: 28 miles.
Journey time: approximately 6-7 hours.

Route Description
The easy ride from Wiveliscombe to Langley precedes a long climb to the summit at Maundown. Thereafter the journey moves into the remote and beautiful area between Huish Champflower and Wimbleball Lake. This is excellent cycling territory but with relatively few places for refreshments it is advisable to carry enough food and drink for the whole journey.

Brompton Regis is the last village of any size and the George Inn the last 'watering hole' before Waterrow as the tour heads for the heights above the valley of the River Exe. The view across the valley towards Dulverton,during the descent towards the A396, must rank as one of the most beautiful in this series of tours.

From the floor of the valley of the River Exe the route climbs round a spur of land before dropping into the neighbouring valley of the River Haddeo and the hamlet of Bury. Here there is a choice and a challenge – to cross the River Haddeo by the ford or by the packhorse bridge. The journey then plunges back into the remote and narrow lanes to Skilgate, Blackmoor (near the Somerset/Devon border), Raddington and Waterrow. The final stage of the ride makes use of farmsteads as guiding markers from Waterrow to Wiveliscombe. This tour is more suited to the regular rider rather than the beginner.

Start: (O.S. Landranger sheet 181, Grid reference ST081276)
From the car park in North Street, Wiveliscombe turn right into North Street and ride towards Langley Marsh. The road passes through Northgate and bears sharply to the left in Langley before long climb up through Langley Marsh past the Three Horse Shoes Inn to just beyond the Maundown Water Treatment Centre.
Points of interest
Wiveliscombe: a pleasant village in the foothills of the Brendon Hills.

Stage 1 Langley Marsh – Huish Champflower – Cuckold's Combe
There is now a steep descent to the River Tone. Cross the the bridge and

A Circular Tour from Wiveliscombe to Wimbleball Lake

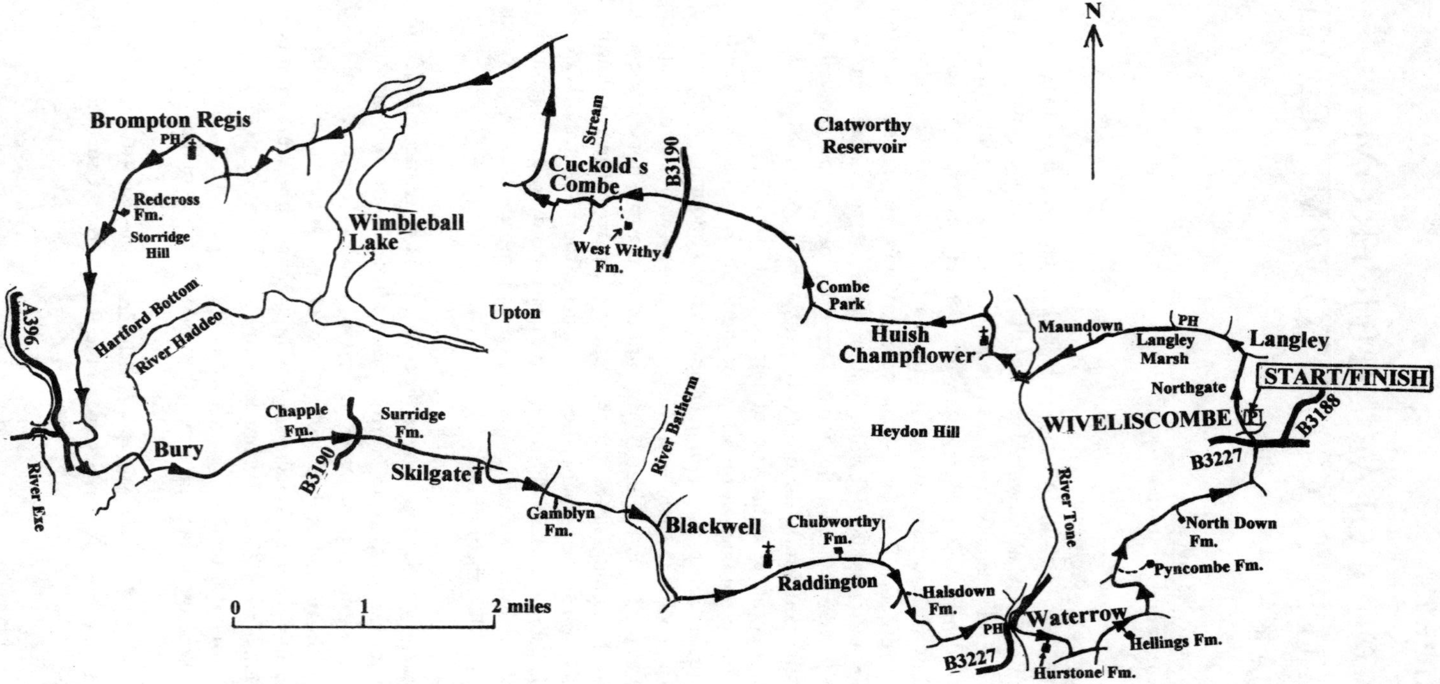

follow the signposted direction to Clatworthy Reservoir uphill past the turning to Huish Moor and over the summit to Huish Champflower. After the church of St Peter take the first turn on the left towards Upton. Continue on, passing Combe Park, down in the valley on the right, before dropping down to a T-junction. Turn right and pass Winters Cottage and at the fork take the signposted road left to Upton. The road descends to the B3190. Cross directly towards Brompton Regis passing West Withy Farm before descending the steep hill to the bottom of Cuckold's Combe.

Points of interest

Huish Champflower: a charming little village beside the River Tone.

Stage 2 Cuckold's Combe – Brompton Regis – Bury

Cross the stream and climb up the side of the combe to a sharp left-hand turn opposite a farm gate. Take the next turn on the right (signposted) to Brompton Regis (3.5 miles), and at the next junction turn right towards Withiel Florey, a delightfully isolated stretch of flat road with wonderful views over the Brendon Hills. At the next T-junction turn left to Brompton Regis (3.5 miles). Wimbleball Lake can be seen soon after joining the road. At the next signpost keep straight on to Brompton Regis (2.5 miles) crossing the bridge over the northern end of the lake.

Keep straight on past the turn to the 'Lake and Water Park' and follow the road to a 1-in-5 drop round a hairpin S-bend and on to a crossroads. Turn right into the village of Brompton Regis. Follow the road which bears round to the rear of the church and passes the George Inn and bears to the left to leave the village. Ignore the turn to the left at Redcross Farm and at the next signposted junction bear left to Dulverton. A descent to the River Exe and the A396 begins near Barlynch Wood with Dulverton clearly visible through the gap between the hills across the valley. Just before the A396 turn left along a minor road which climbs and bears left before dropping down to the River Haddeo and Bury. Cross the river either by using the ford or the packhorse bridge. The ford has a new concrete base and at low water should be quite manageable.

Points of interest

Wimbleball Lake: set in the Exmoor National Park. Completed in 1977 it offers facilities which include fishing, sailing, picnic areas, nature trails and refreshments.

Brompton Regis: a village set high up on Exmoor.

Bury: a remote but charming village with a ford and packhorse bridge across the River Haddeo.

Stage 3 Bury – Skilgate – Blackwell – Raddington – Waterrow – Wiveliscombe

At the next junction turn left towards Skilgate (3 miles) passing Chapple Farm on the left. At the B3190 keep straight on towards Skilgate (1.5 miles) passing Surridge Farm, and at the next junction turn right into the village. Continue through the village to a crossroads keeping straight on towards Raddington (2.5 miles), passing Gamblyn Farm. Cross the River Batherm and bear right into Blackwell. Leave the village and turn left at the next junction, near a post box. The narrow road passes along the valley to Raddington, a small hamlet, identified by the church with a red coloured tower that stands over to the left on the hillside.

The road bears round a sweeping right hand bend at Chubworthy Farm and at a junction at a triangle of land take the road to Waterrow. At a fork take the left-hand road passing the entrance to Halsdown Farm before dropping down to a junction. Turn left and ride down a steep hill to another junction. Turn right to the B3227. The Rock Inn stands near this junction.

Turn left onto the B3227, cross the bridge over the River Tone and then turn immediately right, passing the Hurstone Country Hotel and Restaurant. At a T-junction turn left and at the next crossroads turn left again towards Wiveliscombe. Climb the hill past Hellings Farm and take the first turn on the left. This road wends its way round the rim of a valley. Ignore any turnings to the left and continue along the road passing the entrance to North Down Farm, before dropping down to the next junction. Turn left into Wiveliscombe and at the traffic lights at the B3227 keep straight on up the High Street. Bear left into the Square and right down North Street past the Bear Inn to the car park. The Country Fayre in the High Street provides a wide variety of refreshments and is popular with cyclists. Other places for refreshments are the Bear Inn and the White Hart Inn.

RIDE 24

A CIRCULAR TOUR FROM MINEHEAD TO PORLOCK

Distance: 24 miles.
Journey time: (including the visit to Porlock Weir) approximately 6-7 hours.

Route Description
The high coastline of Exmoor, the heather clad moors, the wooded valleys and the villages combine together in a memorable ride. The route follows minor roads of different gradients and quality of surface as it passes through the villages of Selworthy, Allerford and Bossington before reaching Porlock and Porlock Weir. The return journey through West Luccombe, Luccombe, Wootton Courtenay and Dunster maintains the variation and sustains interest to the end. There are steep uphill sections which may require the rider to dismount and walk, and also steep descents where care should be taken.

Start: (O.S. Landranger sheet 181, Grid reference SS967463)
From the car park in Martlet Road Minehead, turn right into Martlet Road and right again at Blenheim Road. Continue to the junction with the Parade (i.e.the main road through the town). Turn right and ride through the town past the Midland Bank on the left, through the traffic lights and bear right onto the A39 to Porlock. This area is called 'The Parks'. Turn right at Woodcombe Lane which is signposted just short of the speed limit sign on the A39. The road rises through a built-up area with bungalows on the left. Continue and bear left into Bratton Lane, up a hill and away from the residential area to a speed limit sign. The road falls steeply to a farm (Bratton Court). Turn left towards Bratton and pass through the farmyard, across a shallow ford to a fork. Take the right hand to the A39.
Points of interest
Minehead: see Ride 21.

Stage 1 Woodcombe – Selworthy – Allerford – Lynch – Bossington – Porlock
Turn right along the A39 and at the next crossroads turn right to East Lynch. There is a sign stating that the road is unsuitable for motor vehicles. Follow the road and at the next fork take the signposted direction to Selworthy. Continue and at the next junction bear left down the narrow lane. Within a short distance the village of Selworthy is seen. The National Trust

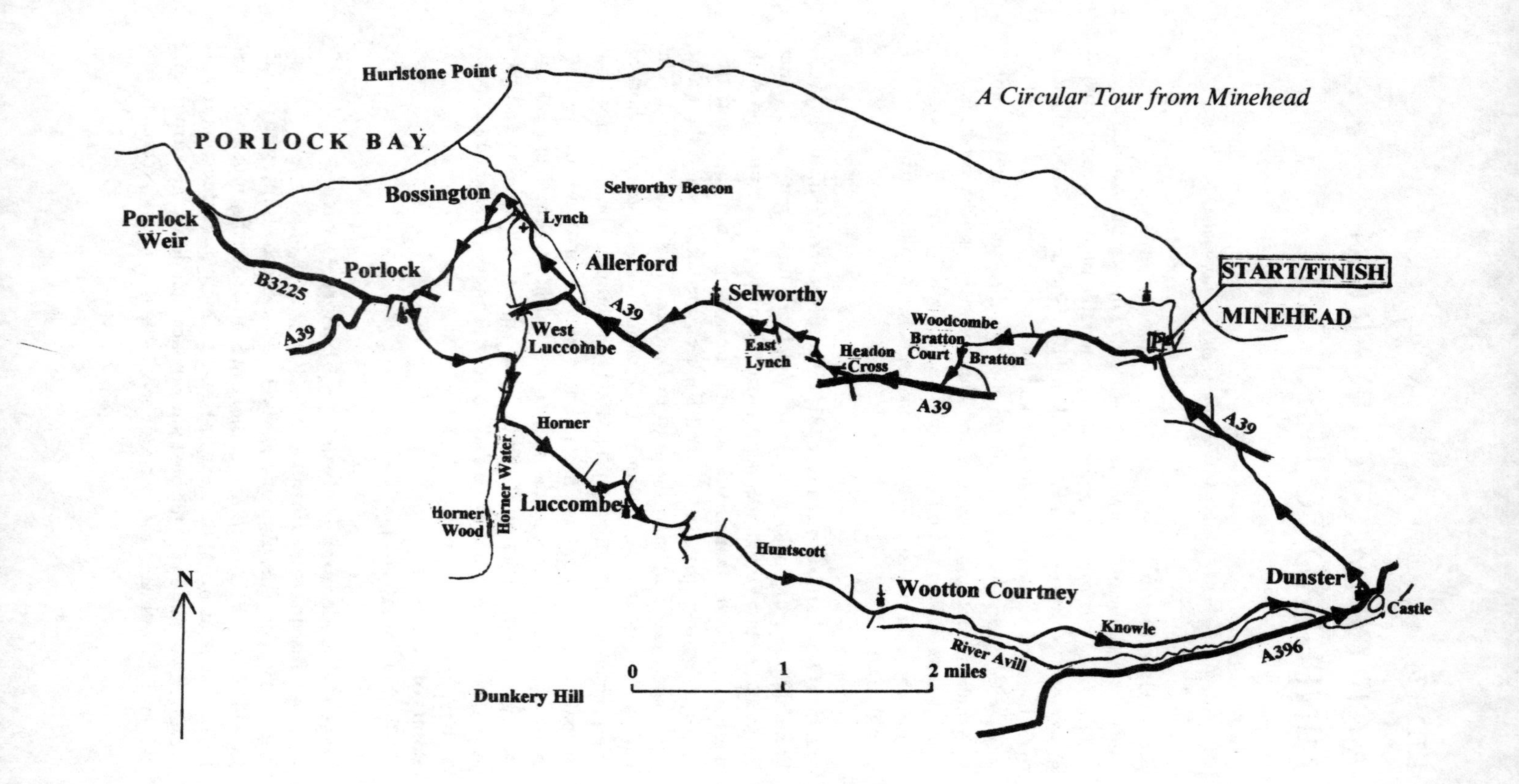
A Circular Tour from Minehead
Hurlstone Point
PORLOCK BAY
Bossington
Selworthy Beacon
Porlock
Weir
Lynch
Allerford
Porlock
B3225
A39
West
Luccombe
A39
Selworthy
START/FINISH
MINEHEAD
Woodcombe
Bratton
Court
Bratton
East
Lynch
Headon
Cross
A39
A39
Horner
Horner Water
Horner
Wood
Luccombe
Huntscott
Wootton Courtney
Dunster
Castle
Knowle
River Avill
A396
N
0
1
2 miles
Dunkery Hill

car park is on the right at the entrance to the village. On leaving Selworthy pass the church and Selworthy Farm before rejoining the A39. Turn right and follow the road to a sharp left-hand bend. Turn right to Allerford. Pass into the village and turn left just before the packhorse bridge. Continue to Lynch passing the Farm Park and a medieval Chapel of Ease. Turn left over the river bridge to a triangle of grass and bear right to Bossington.

The road passes in a left-handed loop through the village with excellent views of Porlock Bay. Leave the village and the next junction turn right and follow this road into Porlock. There are a number of places where refreshments can be obtained along the main street of the town.

Points of interest

Selworthy (NT): famed for its picturesque thatched cottages with their tall rounded chimneys. It is an idyllic village complete with a village green and set against a wooded hillside beneath Selworthy Beacon.

Allerford: a charming village with a much admired packhorse bridge.

Lynch: the medieval Chapel of Ease dating back to 1530 is thought to be the memorial chapel of the Manor of Bossington, which had been in the possession of the Abbey of Athelney since 920.

Bossington: a beautiful village which attracts many visitors.

Porlock: a delightful and bustling old village with Saxon origins, superbly set on the edge of Exmoor and the last habitation on the coast road from Somerset into Devon. The oldest building is the 15th century Doverhay Manor which is now a Museum and Information Centre.

Stage 2 Porlock Weir

Visit to Porlock Weir. Ride through Porlock past the Castle Hotel and at a fork by a shop called the Real McCoy, take the (B3225) to the right to Porlock Weir. Refreshments can be obtained from the Ship Inn or Anchor Hotel.

The journey to Porlock Weir and back to Porlock is 4 miles.

Points of interest

Porlock Weir: this ancient port with its well-known Ship Inn and attractive buildings is now a popular tourist spot.

Stage 3 Porlock – West Luccombe – Luccombe – Wootton Courtenay

Continue from Porlock to West Luccombe by returning along the main street past the Castle Hotel and then bearing left past the church. Take the first turn on the right after the church up Doverhay Road. This narrow road climbs up between very old houses. Bear left to West Luccombe at the signpost on the triangular piece of grass. This is a steep hill which passes round a sharp S-bend before it flattens out briefly at the next signpost. Take the road to the left which falls away quite steeply into the valley, over a cattle-grid and round a sharp right-hand bend into West Luccombe. Cross the packhorse bridge over the stream called Horner Water and continue to Horner. In Horner bear left to Luccombe and at the next crossroads go straight ahead towards Luccombe and Minehead (5 miles). The road turns sharply to the left and at a signpost bear right to Luccombe and Wootton Courtenay.

Continue straight through Luccombe passing the church and Post Office on the right. The road winds its way to Huntscott and on to a Give Way sign. Join the road from the left and go straight on into the village of Wootton Courtenay.

Points of interest

West Luccombe: a pleasant village where a packhorse bridge crosses Horner Water, which cascades down from Dunkery Beacon on its way to Porlock Bay. Look out for the second packhorse bridge in the hamlet of Horner.

Luccombe: the name 'Luccombe' means a 'closed-in combe'. It is a beautiful hamlet of thatched cottages complete with tall chimneys. The house opposite the church is dated 1680. The partly 13th century church is the focal point of the village.

Stage 4 Wootton Courtenay – Dunster – Minehead

Leave Wootton Courtenay passing the church on the left and travel towards Dunster. Ignore all roads to the left and right and keep straight ahead. The road runs parallel to the A396 and the River Avill passing through the hamlet of Knowle to A396 and Dunster.

On the outskirts of Dunster and just before the traffic lights turn left up St George Street, a minor road which bypasses the main part of the village and avoids riding along the A39 into Minehead. The road passes a school on the left and rises, passing a cross on the right.

At the next junction bear left (Combeland Road) and follow the road to the outskirts of Minehead, down Church Street to the A39. Turn left and at the mini-roundabout, bear right down Alcombe Road into the centre of town. Turn right along the Parade to the car park in Martel Road.

Points of interest

Dunster: see Ride 21.

RIDE 25

EXMOOR AND TARR STEPS

Distance: 28 miles.
Journey time: approximately 6-7 hours.

Route Description
Exmoor is quite unlike any other part of Somerset with its deep wooded valleys, remote villages, high rolling hills and the bracken and heather covered moorland. Dulverton, 'the gateway to Exmoor', is the starting point for this ride and there is little time before the stiff climb to Stockham, high above the valley of the River Exe. From this point on, the route through the Exe valley to Exton and onto the hills around and above Winsford includes all types of terrain. The run to Exford goes north onto the moor before turning south to Withypool and Hawkridge. Tarr Steps provides the means of crossing the River Barle and the homeward journey back to Dulverton.

This is not a ride for the beginner and will provide a test for the regular rider.

Start: (O.S. Landranger sheet 181, Grid reference SS912276)
Turn left at the exit to the car park near the river bridge in Dulverton, ride up the main street, bear right by the Chemist's shop and follow the B3222 towards Minehead. Leave the B3222 at the Rock House Inn, in Dulverton, and take the narrow lane to the left of the inn. The lane rises steeply for 0.5 miles to Hollam and then round a sharp right-hand bend to the summit. Continue to Stockham (indicated by a sign on the side of the road) and descend steeply, round a sharp-right hand bend near Halscombe Farm, to the valley bottom and the A396 at Chilly Bridge.

Points of interest
Dulverton: a charming village of mainly 18th century buildings on the River Barle at the southern edge of Exmoor. It is referred to in R.D. Blackmore's book *Lorna Doone*, whose statue stands near Exmoor House, once the workhouse and now the headquarters of the Exmoor National Park Authority.

Stage 1 Chilly Bridge – Exton – Winsford – Exford
Turn left at Chilly Bridge and take the first turn on the right towards Brompton Regis. Pass Stags Head Farm and climb up to a crossroads at the top.

Turn left towards Wheddon Cross and Minehead. Continue along this

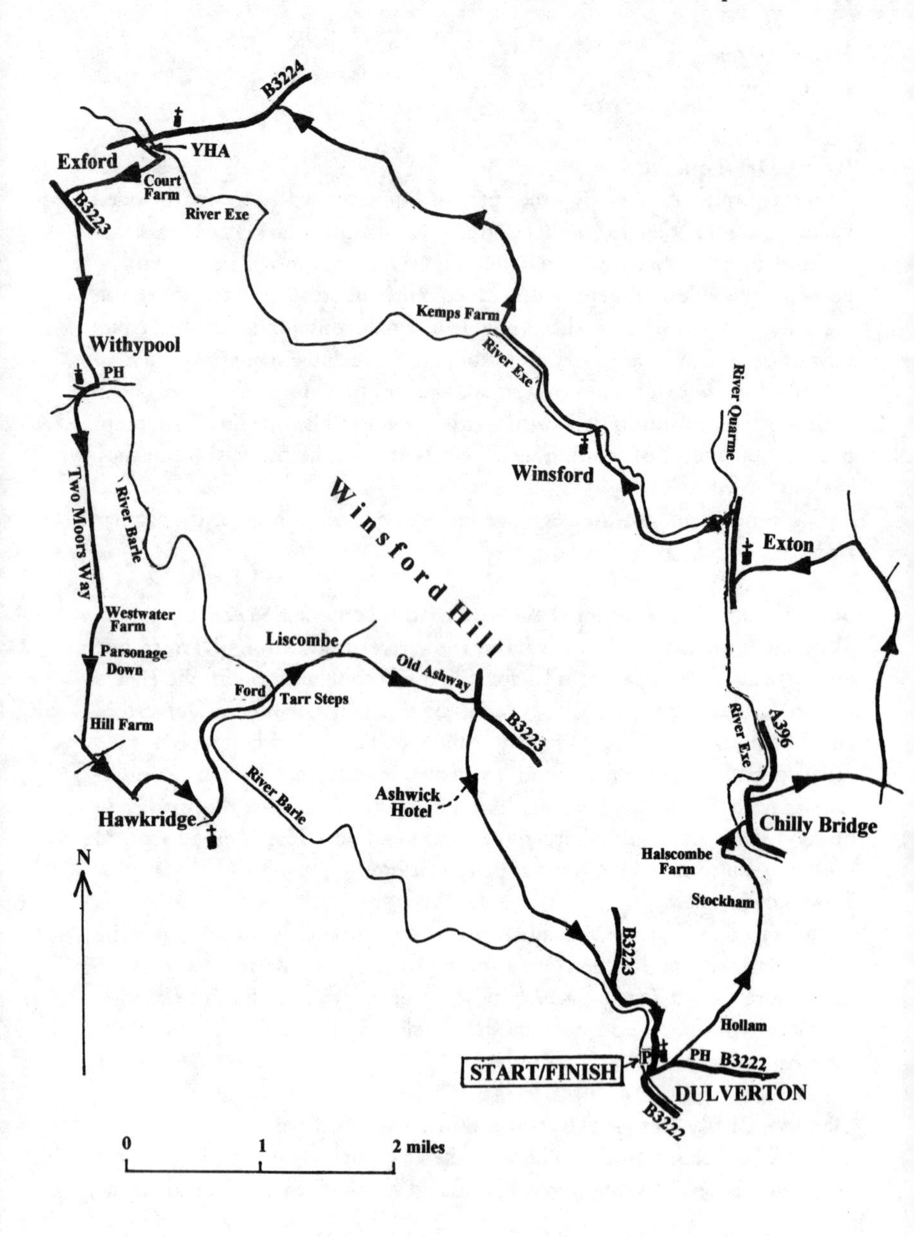
B3224
YHA
Exford
Court Farm
B3223
River Exe
Kemps Farm
River Exe
Withypool
PH
River Quarme
Winsford
Winsford Hill
Two Moors Way
River Barle
Exton
Westwater Farm
Parsonage Down
Liscombe
Old Ashway
Ford
Tarr Steps
B3223
A396
River Exe
Hill Farm
Ashwick Hotel
Hawkridge
River Barle
Chilly Bridge
N
Halscombe Farm
Stockham
B3223
Hollam
START/FINISH
P
PH
B3222
DULVERTON
B3222
0
1
2 miles

flat, hedge-lined road, and take the first turn on the left to Exton (1 mile). The descent into Exton is down a 1-in-4 gradient and care has to be taken, particularly where the road runs steeply round a blind left-hand bend before reaching the A396. Some riders may feel happier walking down this final section.

Turn right at the A396 and ride along the valley bottom and take the first turn on the left to Winsford (1.5 miles), Withypool (5.25 miles) and Exford. The River Exe and the River Quarme meet near this point. Cross the River Exe and follow the river to Winsford. The village is charming and full of interest and an appropriate place to have a break. Refreshments can be obtained from either the Royal Oak Inn or the nearby Karslake House Hotel. These two hostelries are on the road to the left of the War Memorial. From Winsford continue along the valley past Kemps Farm (on the left) where the road bears sharply to the right and away from the River Exe to continue its snaking path alongside Larcombe Brook to the B3224. Turn left to Exford (1 mile).

The road passes a church on the outskirts of Exford before dropping down a 1-in-6 hill into the village. At the triangle with the numerous signposts keep to the left opposite the Crown Hotel. Pass the Exmoor Lodge on the right, cross the bridge near the White Horse Inn on the right, and turn left immediately passing the Youth Hostel on the left.

Points of interest

Exton: high up overlooking the Exe valley.

Winsford: said to be the most attractive village on Exmoor. It has several packhorse bridges and a lovely old thatched Royal Oak Inn. The 15th century church has some Norman features. Ernest Bevin was born here in 1881.

Stage 2 Exford – Withypool – Hawkridge – Tarr Steps – Dulverton

From the Youth Hostel climb to a sharp right-hand bend at the entrance to Court Farm and on to the B3223. Turn left and then take the first on the right along a road marked 'Unsuitable for Heavy Goods Vehicles'. This is a flat road with a good surface from which there are excellent views over the moors. It eventually descends a 1-in-5 gradient into Withypool. The church of St Andrew is away to the right. Turn right at the junction with the main road through the village, pass the church, bear left across the River Barle. Bear left again up the hill to the moors above.

This section of the route, the Two Moors Way, overlooks Withypool and the River Barle and provides extensive views over Exmoor. This flat road eventually descends to Westwater Farm and climbs up Parsonage Down. Pass the entrance to Hill Farm and at the next road junction bear left to Hawkridge (1.25 miles) and Dulverton (5.25 miles). Keep straight on at the first turning on the left to Tarr Steps. Turn left at the signpost to Hawkridge, follow a curving right hand bend to a junction near a large tree with a seat fixed around its trunk.

Turn left and follow the signposted direction to Tarr Steps which passes the church before turning down a narrow, well-surfaced lane and 1-in-4 hill. The initial part of the downhill journey is the steepest and the gradient improves as it passes through a wood. To cross the ford it is necessary to either push or carry the bicycle across the 'steps' or to wade across when the water level is low.

From Tarr Steps follow the road which climbs steeply from the River Barle passing a public car park on the right. Continue to the fork at Liscombe and take the road to the right which descends along Old Ashway to the B3223. Ride to another fork and bear right along this quiet alternative route to Dulverton. The road descends past the Ashwick Hotel, its steepness increasing as it approaches valley bottom and the B3223. Turn right to Dulverton and continue beside the river through the delightful outskirts of Dulverton to the B3222 and from there to the car park.

Points of interest

Withypool: a pretty village on the River Barle.

Hawkridge: a quiet little hamlet high on a ridge above the Barle.

Tarr Steps: an ancient ford over the River Barle; the exact date of the old stone clapper bridge is unknown.

Bicycle Shops, Repairs and Hire

Burnham-on-Sea	G.H. Cycle Centre 19 High Street	0278 782350
Castle Cary	Bernie Hockey Cycles Torbay Road (Hire)	0963 50559
Chard	Chard Cycle Company 16 Holyrood Street	0460 62474
Crewkerne	Bicycle World 35 South Street	0460 76822
Frome	P. J. Cycles 9 The Bridge	0373 453563
Ilminster	Miller (Cycles) The Old Bakery Shudrick Lane	0460 57015
Langport	Franks Auto Needs and Cycles North Street (Hire)	0458 250348
Merriott	Stennings Merriottsford Garage	0460 75089
Minehead	Minehead Cycles Market House The Parade	0643 706728
	Pompy's Cycles Mart Road (Hire)	0643 704077
Porlock	Porlock Hardware High Street	0643 862427
Shepton Mallet	Dave Hockey The Power House Waterloo Road	0749 342154

Street	On Your Bike 128A High Street (Hire)	0458 43048
Taunton	Ralph Colman 79 Station Road (Hire)	0823 275822
Wellington	Kings Cycles 7 Cornhill	0823 662260
Wells	City Cycles 80 High Street	0749 675096
Wrington (Avon)	Richards Broad Street	0934 862278
Yeovil	Yeovil Cycle Centre 8-10 South Western Terrace (Hire)	0935 22000
	PDE Cycles 72 Wessex Road	0935 72151

Tourist Information Centres

Bridgwater	Town Hall 50 High Street	0278 427652 (Summer only)
Burnham-on-Sea	South Esplanade	0278 787852
Chard	Guildhall Fore Street	0460 67463
Cheddar Gorge	The Gorge	0934 744071
Dulverton	High Street	0398 23841 (Summer only)
Dunster	Exmoor National Park Centre Steep Car Park	0643 821835 (Summer only)
Frome	The Round Tower Justice Lane	0373 467271 (Summer only)
Glastonbury	The Tribunal 9 High Street	0458 832954 (Summer only)
Ilminster	Shudrick Lane	0460 57294 (Summer only)
Minehead	17 Friday Street	0634 702624 (All year)
Shepton Mallet	2 Petticoat Lane	0749 325258 (Summer only)
Somerset Visitor Centre	Sedgemoor Services M5 Motorway (between Exits 21and 22)	0934 750833 (All year)
Taunton	The Library Corporation Street	0823 274785 (All year)
Watchet	6 The Esplanade	

Wellington	Wellington Museum 28 Fore Street	0823 664747 (Summer only)
Wells	Town Hall Market Place	0749 672552
Wincanton	The Library 7 Carrington Way	0963 34063 (All year)
Yeovil	Petter's Way	0935 71279